BATTLE *of the* BLUES

The Oxford & Cambridge Boat Race from 1829

Christopher Dodd & John Marks

*Above and front cover:
Crews passing Thorneycrofts,
Cambridge leading, 1902*

*Left: the Oxford and Cambridge
Boat Race, showing two eights
stroked on bow or starboard
side (historically inaccurate)
lithograph by Lipschitz, c1871*

1 *Cambridge after crossing the line first in 1907*

2 *Oxford, 1891*

3 *First Boat Race programme, 1929*

4 *Oxford's Leviathon, 1951*

5 *Cambridge, 1932*

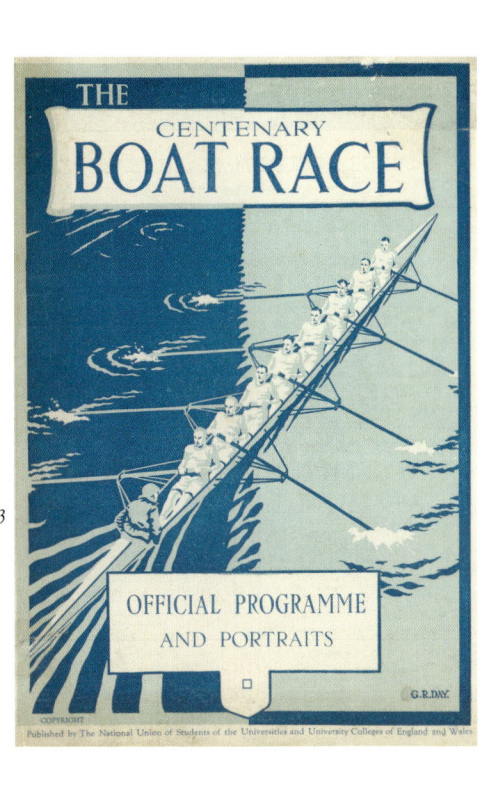

BATTLE OF THE BLUES

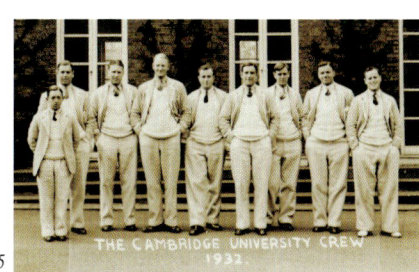

Contents

5	A private match for public consumption	*Hugh Matheson*
11	The first Boat Race	*Christopher Dodd*
12	1830 to 1855: Fits and starts	*John Marks*
19	An Oxford boat with a Cornish accent	*Mark Edwards*
25	Weather plays a merry dance	*Daniel Topolski*
28	1856 to 1883: Oxford take the lead	*John Marks*
37	How to peak on the right day	*Donald Legget*
38	1884 to 1914: Floreat Etona	*John Marks*
43	The umpire takes charge	*Mike Sweeney*
51	Stage setting and management	*Duncan Clegg*
54	1920 to 1939: Light Blues fight back	*John Marks*
57	Mutiny tests loyalty	*Hugh Matheson*
62	1940 to 1945: Wartime races	*John Marks*
64	1946 to 1975: Swings of fortune	*John Marks*
69	Getting the news out	*Christopher Dodd*
78	The Light Blue Lauries	*Hugh Laurie*
81	In camera	*Barbara Slater*
82	1946 to 1975: Isis and Goldie join the party	*John Marks*
84	1976 to 2003: Battles of the giants	*John Marks*
87	Trail blazing imagery	*Thomas E Weil*
100	Blues from 1946 to 2003	
106	Oxford versus Cambridge from 1829	
107	Bibliography and sources	

SATURDAY MARCH 31ST - 9·45 AM

NEAREST STATIONS:- PUTNEY BRIDGE, HAMMERSMITH
RAVENSCOURT Pk, TURNHAM GREEN & CHISWICK Pk

UndergrounD

4 BATTLE OF THE BLUES

In 1857 Oxford won in Matt Taylor's boat, the first keel-less, in 22 mins 35 secs. Matt Taylor himself came down to tell them how to row her, his entire personal luggage consisting of some brushes and a pot of varnish in a red handkerchief.

Theodore Cook in the
John Buchan Annual, 1921

1   London Transport poster, 1928

2   The 1829 gold sovereign used for the toss for stations

A private match for public consumption   HUGH MATHESON

The rules for the boat race refer with satisfying clarity to 'either' university. No grappling here with twenty-first century inclusiveness. The boat race decides which is best of two with a precise and objective result, arrived at almost without the intervention of any technological device.

As an ancient institution it breezes through the simple test: If you started today would you make it in the same way? The answer from the oarsmen, the swathe of spectators on the bank and the media is 'yes'. If you had the wit, you would. Vice-chancellors don't ask why we choose to indulge in this exclusive private match; they only get quarrelsome when their set of blues don't win.

The boat race has survived the enormous social change that has transformed Oxford and Cambridge universities in every other way over the past 175 years. It continues to project the same qualities of fair play that it adopted in its infancy, and once a year it demonstrates publicly the cut and thrust of the eternal rivalry between the two elite academic institutions – a rivalry known to blues as 'the needle'.

Because it is rowed over a peculiar, twisting course in enormously variable conditions and without the help of drugs or diesel by crews all of who are in 'statu pupilari', the boat race seems to the outsider looking in as if nothing has changed. Nine against nine, with eight on each side presenting the suffering, glazed look of galley slaves and two hyperactive Chihuahuas barking from the stern. The spectators are wisely informed that the bodies are bigger and fitter and the boats and oars are wonders of carbon fibre technology. But it still looks the same.

BATTLE OF THE BLUES   **5**

1 *Boat Race fans, 1890*

2 *The Spurt, 1878*

Two pretty symphonies in blue.

To the untutored eye the boats used in the first Putney to Mortlake race in 1845 are barely distinguishable from the slender shells which have covered the four and a quarter miles in less than 17 minutes. The same untutored voice sometimes does claim, quite inaccurately, that the race is no longer the same because it has been taken over by American postgraduates and is therefore no longer a contest between true Oxford and Cambridge.

A more considered view would note that the race has always imposed the same physical demands, with a burst of explosive strength needed off the start (and in the past few years at the finish) followed by four miles of endurance strength or stamina rowing. While the explosive muscle fibre can be put on in the gymnasium at almost any age, the endurance strength comes more slowly and with long hours of training. From the beginning, boat race crews were made up mostly from final year men and when gradually more and more stayed up for four years and more, they tended to be selected for their greater stamina, a process which reached its apogee when Boris Rankov of Bradford Grammar School won six blues on the trot while he dwelt on the use of the Roman spear in first century Macedonia.

Since the cost of university became free to British students after the 1939-45 world war, there has been a huge increase in postgraduate students from abroad who pay for their tuition and present themselves with more endurance fitness than the tender home-grown undergraduates. Sometimes they possess more ingrained oar handling skills. So the number of foreign postgraduates aspiring and qualified to row in the race has increased sharply since 1945. This influx has had little peaks explained by quite other reasons. European universities were useful places to be while the Americans were drafting all males of fighting age to wage war in Vietnam, and crowds of them found their way to Oxford in the company of future US president, Bill Clinton.

6 BATTLE OF THE BLUES

The very many thousands who will assemble this afternoon on the banks of the Thames for the boat race, and at Crystal Palace, Sydenham, for the final tie of the Football Association Cup, provide ample proof of the internal peace of the kingdom.

The Graphic, 30 March, 1895

In the 1990s as vice-chancellors spread their nets ever wider in the spirit of global scholarship but with a weather eye on the fee income, we had the first blues from Germany, Italy, Netherlands, Norway and Sweden as well as a continuing flow from Commonwealth countries and the United States. Several blues have found their way to the boat race from former Yugoslavia via a British or American education. In many cases oarsmen of all nationalities were stepping back and forth between boat race and international duties, often hiding from their academic tutors the massive extra workload they were carrying. For every blue who has burned out, unable to take the strain, there has been another who wins the boat race, takes a first class degree, and caps it all with an Olympic medal.

To counterbalance this acknowledgement that the race is a feat of endurance and learned skills are several recent examples of young undergraduates lowering the bar on participation. Matthew Brittin is the youngest ever at 18 years 208 days when he won a Cambridge blue in 1987, and Matthew Smith of Oxford was a few days older in 2001. Both learned to row and excel academically at Hampton School.

By chance Hampton spawned two sets of brothers who opposed each other in the 2003 race, with Smith's younger brother Ben rowing for Cambridge, and the Livingston brothers James and Dave representing Cambridge and Oxford respectively.

In the 1980s both universities abandoned their habit of using mostly old blue, amateur coaches in a fortnightly roster under the aegis of one head coach who would take the final two weeks on the tideway in favour of full-time professional coaching teams.

There's a living thread that goes winding, winding,

Tortuous rather, but easy of finding,

   Creep and crawl

   By paling and wall –

Very much like a dust-dry snake –

From Hyde Park Corner right out to Mortlake;

   Crawl and creep

   By level and steep,

From Hammersmith Bridge back again to Eastcheap, -

   Horse and man,

   Wagon and van,

Jog-trotting along since the day began –

Rollicking, rumbling and rolling apace,

With their heads all one way like a shoal of dace;

   And beauty and grace,

   And the Mayor without mace,

   Silk satins and lace,

   And the evil in case,

Seem within an ace of a cultural embrace,

   As if the whole place

   Had set its whole face

To see the Oxford and Cambridge Race.

H Cholmondeley-Pennell, Puck on Pegasus, 1874

1 Oxford's carte de visite, 1882

2 The Boat Race at Mortlake, 1868

The lure of a place in the blue boat glisters in the waters where these people learn their rowing. It is transmitted round a small world, in which the universities are accessible to all with the brains to obtain a place and the money to pay for their academic education. Those with the capacity to take a masters degree and win a blue would be mad to settle for less. Many of them know the reputations of the chief coaches, and often say they came to spend a year or two in the boat race system as a key step on their way to the Olympic podium.

At the same time, provided you can endure the grinding work on the water and in the gym, you can join this elite with a fraction of the pure athletic talent it would take to win an Olympic medal in any other front line sport.

And it all comes in a package which cannot be defined. The experience is diverse and can mean such different things in dark blue or light blue colours, but if you can take pleasure in the pressure and thrive in such an intensity of competition and public interest, then the rest of life can seem a breeze. Now that's an education worth fighting for.

BATTLE OF THE BLUES 9

The Oxford and Cambridge Rowing Match at Henley-on-Thames, 1829

Before the first race in 1829 Charles Merivale wrote to his mother to caution her 'not to believe an advertisement which is to be seen in some of the papers about the match being for £500. It is not an exaggeration even, but a lie.'

The first Boat Race CHRISTOPHER DODD

Wednesday 10 June 1829: At ten minutes past eight in the evening a shout filled the lush green valley between the wood-crowned hills at Henley-on-Thames, a din unsurpassed in the lifetime of the reporter from London Society who witnessed its ignition. An eight-oared crew from the University of Oxford had just beaten its rival from Cambridge from Hambleden lock to Henley bridge, a distance of two and a quarter miles against the stream, by about sixty yards in 14 minutes and 30 seconds. 'It has never fallen to my lot to hear such a shout since. There was fierce applause at the installation of the Duke of Wellington a few years after, but applause that fills a valley is a different thing,' he wrote.

The race had attracted a huge throng – some accounts say 20,000 – on a balmy summer evening, the majority from Oxford, which was 23 miles away by horseback, gig, tandem, pair, four-horse drag or stage. Hundreds wearing the dark blue favours of Oxford or the pink of Cambridge took to the towpath or crushed on to the bridge to witness Oxford emerge from the narrow channel on the Berkshire side of Temple eyot and take a lead up the mile-long straight. The square tower of St Mary's parish church stood like a lighthouse at the end of it, beckoning coxswain William Fremantle. Tumult broke out as the boat rounded the point where the poplar trees stood and crossed the finish line downstream of Henley's elegant, five-arched bridge, with Cambridge trailing home five or six boat lengths behind.

1830 to 1855

FITS AND STARTS

After such a dramatic and successful start, the boat race became a national institution which has now flourished for 175 years, but its early development was a bumpy ride.

The Oxford and Cambridge contest was originally conceived as a private match between two crews of nine students, not as a public exhibition. Thus it remains to the present day. This largely explains why there were only twelve official races from 1829 to 1855 inclusive, and that it was not until 1856 that the boat race became an annual event, interrupted only by world wars from 1915 to 1919 and 1940 to 1945.

Sports in both Oxford and Cambridge are organised by the students, not by the university. Indeed for much of the time there has been active discouragement of sport from college and university authorities intent on academic excellence. To start up and, more importantly, to maintain a new inter-university sporting venture requires an annual succession of enthusiastic students at each university. The history of most inter-university sports is of early difficulties and failures. Since this is still the situation in an age of rapid communication and transport, how much more student enthusiasm was required in the first half of the 1800s.

Moreover, the autonomous collegiate nature of Oxford and Cambridge universities makes the negotiation of inter-university competition more difficult, for the university clubs are governed by the student presidents of college boat clubs, all with their own agendas.

Thus one should ascribe the long early periods between races largely to the inherent difficulties of the system rather than protracted squabbling between the universities. These included the different dates of the university terms and examinations and hence different availability for training and competition; strong commitment to academic excellence even among the sporting elite; the difficulty in finding a venue which would not favour one university more than the other; the late foundation of the Oxford University Boat Club (1839), and competition with other regattas in Henley and London at which the colleges could enjoy the pleasure of pot-hunting.

1 *Sketches at the first Boat Race by Uncle Peter*

2 *Charles Merivale and*
3 *Charles Wordsworth, founders of the Boat Race. Merivale rowed in the four seat for Cambridge in 1829, and Wordsworth in the same seat for Oxford*

The only really necessary things to be adhered to are moderation in eating, drinking and sleeping. Internal fat is the great enemy of good wind… all will be of no use unless the liquors are cut off, for it is through them that the internal fat is produced and especially by beer.

Arthur Shadwell
in Principles of Rowing 1846

Cambridge had won the toss of a coin to choose the Berkshire shore where the towpath is, giving them the inside station round the three-quarter mile bend which begins shortly after the start and leads to the island, thus adding to their favoured status among spectators and gamblers. Oxford, however, had other ideas. Thomas Staniforth, their stroke, and Stephen Davies, their boat builder and coach, had studied the set of the stream at the island and decided that the towpath channel had far less stream than that on the Buckinghamshire side. To take it therefore required somehow crossing over into Cambridge's water.

This they tried to do. Cambridge did not give way, and there was a clash, Oxford's stroke and six locking oars with Cambridge's bow and three. A restart was ordered. It is not known from where this occurred, but it is likely that the crews returned to the original start. Each crew had appointed an umpire, and there was a referee to arbitrate between the two. Oxford's umpire, Cyril Page, is quoted as declaring that both boats should take the wide, Bucks side of the island, while Cambridge's umpire J Stuart Roupell kept silent because it was Staniforth, and not his own captain, who solicited his opinion. The referee, as far as we know, did not pronounce judgment either. After the second start Oxford ignored their umpire's advice and advanced far enough to pass in front of Cambridge.

Prior to this race, there was growing interest in boat racing at the universities, but no formal contact between them. The first known inter-college race at Oxford was Brasenose versus Jesus in 1815, while at Cambridge, St John's launched the first eight-oar on the Cam in 1826, with college races taking place in 1827. Cambridge University Boat Club was formed in that year, twelve years earlier than its Oxford counterpart.

It is not surprising that the next 26 years (1830 to 1855) saw only eleven official races, although the crews often raced each other at various regattas. (see 'Other skirmishes' page 26).

From 1830 to 1835 efforts were made to fix both a venue and date, but none were agreed. The second race in June 1836 was rowed from Westminster to Putney, the recognised course for other races which took place in London. The race is mainly notable as the first in which both crews sported shades of blue. The story goes that when they assembled for the 1836 race, Oxford were wearing dark blue and white striped jerseys, as in 1829, but Cambridge had no distinguishing colour. A Cambridge supporter, Mr R N Phillips of Christ's College, ran to a shop and bought a length of a light blue Eton ribbon which was attached to the bow of their boat. From then on, Oxford retained its dark blue colour and Cambridge adopted a light blue which is similar to Eton blue. Hence 1836 represented the first 'Battle of the Blues'.

The race was won by Cambridge but the standard of rowing was adversely criticised by both the London watermen and amateur oarsmen on the tideway. Clearly, far too little training was done prior to the race.

1

> *Robert Coombes remembered a man who was rowing in his second university crew: 'I always told him so; and yet he could speak and shout in the middle of a hard trial, when all the rest were done to a whisper. Why, a man who does this dispirits the others.'*
>
> *Robert Coombes, Cambridge's professional coach in the 1840s and early 1850s, Aquatic Notes 1852*

1 Searle & Sons Boatbuilders at Lambeth, showing a variety of rowing craft. The boatyard was a centre for rowing in the early nineteenth century and home to the Cambridge Subscription Rooms

2 Thomas Egan, Cambridge cox 1836, 1839 and 1840 and influential coach

The inter-university race came about because two friends from Harrow school, Charles Wordsworth of Christ Church, Oxford, and Charles Merivale of St John's, Cambridge, met during the vacation in Cambridge, where Wordsworth's father was master of Trinity. Wordsworth went rowing on the Cam, and the two school fellows, probably with others, decided to set up a challenge. Accordingly, on February 20 1829 a meeting of Cambridge University Boat Club requested Mr Snow of St John's to write immediately to Mr Staniforth of Christ Church stating 'that the University of Cambridge hereby challenge the University of Oxford to row a match at or near London, each in an eight-oared boat during the ensuing Easter vacation.'

After considerable correspondence, the time, date and place were agreed. The Cambridge boat is attributed by one source to Logan and another to Searle, both London builders. The Sporting Magazine says it was painted pink, the colour of St John's College, and observed that it 'buried forward' when manned. It was loaned to Westminster School for their first match against Eton later that summer. Oxford borrowed a gig from Balliol that was built by Davies and King of Oxford (see page 19). Jackson's Oxford Journal had a poor opinion of Cambridge's boat: 'though… much gayer in appearance than the old Oxford boat, [the Cambridge boat] was far inferior in the water, dipping to the oar whilst the other rose to every stroke in fine style.' Oxford's boat has survived 175 years and is at the River and Rowing Museum in Henley.

The third race took place during the Easter vacation of 1839, again from Westminster to Putney. Oxford still had no university rowing club, and the crew which they put out was inferior to that from Cambridge, who led from the start and won by over one and a half minutes. A second successive defeat encouraged Oxford to found their club in 1839.

On 15 April 1840 the fourth race was again rowed from Westminster to Putney. Oxford led from the start and maintained their lead for a substantial part of the championship course, but their lack of training eventually let Cambridge overtake them as they came towards Putney Bridge and the light blues won by just under a length from a more coherent Oxford crew than those of previous years.

Grand Match between Oxford and Cambridge, passing Lambeth Palace, 1841

The year 1842 saw a revolution at Oxford when Fletcher Menzies, with the help of Arthur Shadwell, who had gone from St John's, Cambridge, to Balliol, Oxford, put together his own crew, who defeated the university crew, causing Menzies to be elected president. The race was held over the Westminster to Putney course, with the Oxford crew, who had only undertaken training for just over three weeks, winning by three lengths.

These and subsequent races were rowed on a busy river open to heavy traffic during the event. Barges, skiffs and wherries became entangled with racing eights. Traffic was increased by a substantial number of coal-fired steamers carrying supporters and spectators. These not only moored beam to beam alongside the banks but followed or even preceded the eights as they progressed along the course, belching out clouds of acrid smoke.

Contemporary reports give frequent examples of both accidental and deliberate balking of the crews. Thus we read of the 1842 race: 'Shadwell (the Oxford cox) being faced by the jam of the boats as he neared the finish and finding the Leander boat right across his path, stood up in his seat, the better to see his way and, no doubt, to express his views…'

16 BATTLE OF THE BLUES

> By the late 1830s rowing men at Oxford and Cambridge were becoming wary of the attitudes of some of the amateurs of the day. In time they were to convert most of the latter to their point of view, especially those on the metropolitan Thames. This alliance was to be of great import, especially when it was reinforced during the second half of the century by the public schools, increasingly consumed by their passion for athleticism.
>
> Eric Halladay
> in Rowing in England, 1990

On June 2 Oxford changed their crew when Croft of Balliol was taken ill. John Bates of Christ Church was brought in, Thomas Garnier was moved from stroke to six and Staniforth took the stroke seat. Wordsworth described their uniform in a letter to Merivale a few days before the race: 'Black straw hats, dark blue striped jerseys, and canvas trousers.' This was based on the colours of Christ Church, whence came four oarsmen and the cox. Cambridge dressed in white shirts with pink sashes worn round the waist. There were three Trinity men and three from Lady Margaret Boat Club of St John's in the crew. The uniform of the former was a buff jersey with blue stripes, of the latter a white jersey with light pink stripes. The crew could not agree which to wear, so they chose to row in their shirts with pink sashes in compliment to the captain, William Snow, who was a Lady Margaret man.

A rich mixture of adventure and controversy surrounded the first race between Oxford and Cambridge. Jonathan Toogood of Oxford, the heaviest man at over 14 stone, saved his place at Balliol by attending a logic lecture, as required by the college's master, at one o'clock on the day of the race before dashing to Henley. Merivale wrote to his mother in May to scotch a newspaper report that the match was for £500. 'It is not an exaggeration even, but a lie. In fact I have not a sixpence staked thereon.' There were a hundred opinions as to the best course to take between Hambleden and Henley. There was a clash of blades, a foul, a re-start, some vague umpiring decisions, and a riotous finale in the town that night.

Thus competitive boat racing arrived in a small Thames settlement that happens to have the longest stretch of straight water on the upper Thames. Thereafter the boat race, in fits and starts, moved down river to the tidal Thames, but the events of June 10 1829 led to the foundation of a regatta at Henley ten years later. Little did Wordsworth and Merivale realise what they had ignited; much less how recognisable it would be a hundred and seventy five years later.

1   Mark Edwards with his replica of Oxford's 1829 boat

2   Oxford's first boat, borrowed from Balliol College, 1829

- 1841 Oxford lose in a carvel-built eight with planks arranged to form a smooth surface.
- 1845 Cambridge outrigger built in eight days (not used).
- 1846 Both crews use fully out-rigged boats.
- 1857 Oxford win in Matt Taylor's smooth-hulled boat with keel inboard.
- 1873 Both crews use sliding seats.
- 1902 Oxford use swivel rowlocks.
- 1934 Oxford boat built in 72 hours.
- 1960 Oxford use 'spade' blades.
- 1977 Oxford use composite plastic boat.
- 1993 Asymmetrical 'hatchet' blades introduced.

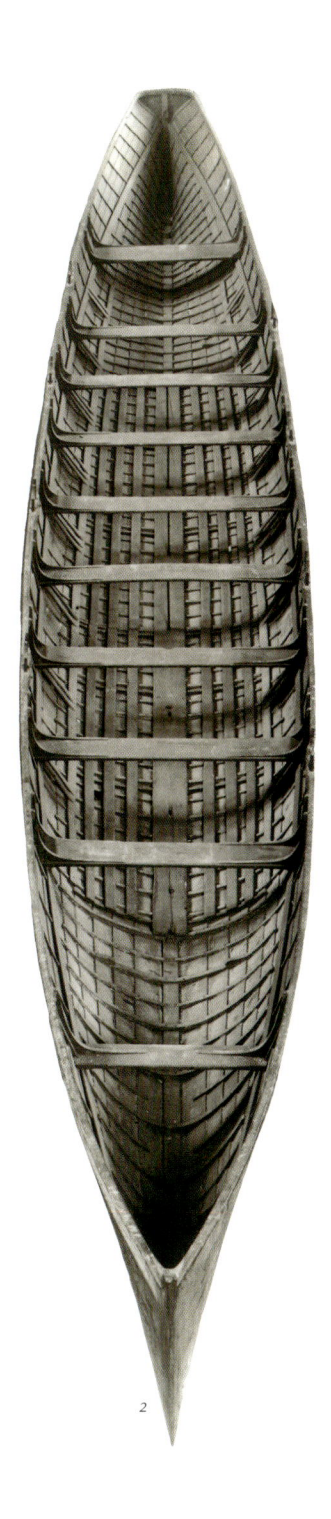

An Oxford boat with a Cornish accent MARK EDWARDS

The boat built for Balliol College by Stephen Davies and Isaac King and used by Oxford in the 1829 boat race owes the vast majority of its design and method of construction to the pilot gigs of Cornwall. Stephen Davies was almost certainly a journeyman boatbuilder, trained possibly by the Peters family of Polwarth, St Mawes, famous for building the fastest pilot gigs from 1790 onward.

The pilot gigs of Cornwall had evolved to row out to sea to meet incoming vessels approaching the English Channel from the Atlantic in order to put a pilot on board. They had to be seaworthy, safe alongside a tossing ship, return home and beach, possibly with a following sea. But most important, they had to be fast. Piloting was a highly competitive business and, as with the boat race, there are only two results – win or lose (excepting 1877).

This inheritance explains the Oxford boat's ten narrow planks a side, giving a flexible hull resistant to the impact of seas, ships and beaches. She has a pronounced sheer, the top line of the boat rising high at the bow and stern, reducing the risk of a sea overwhelming her. The stem is upright with a rounded nose so as not to snag a heaving ship. The hull is strengthened with steamed ribs carefully joggled over the planking in the bilge and spaced only 150mm apart. This gives a light, strong but flexible hull. Each of the eight rowing and single coxswain's thwarts or seats have four strong supportive knees. To produce a seat for the oarsman a moulded wooden pad fills the otherwise uncomfortable gap between the two knees furthest away from the rowlock. A visit to the River and Rowing Museum reveals the same detail in a thwart from the pilot gig Treffry built by William Peters in 1812. The steamed ribs riveted into the hull are in every detail the same as a pilot gig, one from the gunwhale to gunwhale followed 6 inches further on by a shorter floor timber and so on throughout the full 45 ft 4 in hull.

The next official race was in the Easter vacation 1845, and to reduce the interference from heavy river traffic the course was changed to 'Putney bridge to Mortlake church tower'. Cambridge won by thirty seconds (eight or nine lengths).

The following year (1846) a race was again agreed over the same course, but at the last moment it was decided to row it downstream on the ebb tide, a situation which greatly benefited the Middlesex station, with its long favourable bend from the start. Cambridge, on this station, won by three lengths, although Oxford held their rivals for most of the course.

Much of the coaching during this period rested upon the shoulders of professional watermen, and the substantial level of wagers and side bets that prevailed, though probably not among the competitors, encouraged fouling which was an accepted component of racing. For this reason there was an umpire for each crew and a neutral referee. In 1842 the university crews foreswore deliberate fouling, and from then on a single umpire has officiated. A senior, respected old blue, nearly always a past president, has officiated for most races since.

1 *The Oxford and Cambridge Cutter Match off Lambeth Palace, 1842*

2 *Replica of Oxford's 1829 boat by Mark Edwards, Richmond Boathouse, 2004*

The inside of the seat of the trousers may be lined with a large soft skin of washleather to prevent the fibres of the material irritating the cuticle. It has the disadvantage, if much worn, of getting hard after becoming wet from perspiration, or from water coming in over the side of the boat.

The Arts of Rowing and Training, 1866

An Oxford boat with a Cornish accent *continued*

There are of course differences. The Oxford boat is eight-oared rather than the normal six of the pilot gig. West Country gigs were limited by order of H M Customs and Excise so that the revenue boats stood a chance of catching a smuggling suspect. By 1829 eight-oared boats were becoming the norm amongst gentlemen rowers at schools and colleges. The 45 ft length was needed for speed. If it was shorter, the 'waterline length rule' forces the boat to climb its own bow wave; much longer and the greater wetted surface increasingly slows the boat. The ideal length is a compromise related to hull cross section, the boat's weight and, most importantly, the overall power of the crew. The stronger the crew the longer the boat needs to be to reach an optimum speed.

The gig of Stephen Davies must have caused some comment amongst Thames boatbuilders. Almost everything was quite different to a Thames build. On the Thames most boats were built in the Lambeth area where the Scandinavian inheritance of all clinker boats was still retained. There would be only six, maybe seven, planks on each side. The gunwhale would consist of a single board, a saxboard rising up from its lower sheerline to the rowlocks. The stem would be raked with a sharp nose for landing passengers and crew on steps or a foreshore. The hull would be stiffened by heavier timbers sawn to the shape without bending, and only half the number of knees would be used.

1830 to 1855

In 1849, after a gap of two years and for the only time, there were two races. The first in March from Putney to Mortlake was won by Cambridge 'easily'. Oxford felt that their craft was a major factor in their defeat and challenged Cambridge to a further race in December. This is the only time in the series to 2003 that the boat race was decided by a disqualification, following a foul by Cambridge.

The eleventh race in 1852 saw the great Oxonian Joseph Chitty as president and stroke. This race was at the height of the argument which had started in 1846 about the use of professional coaches and steersmen and which was the biggest factor in the decision to settle for amateur coaches (mainly old blues), a decision which held for more than a century. Cambridge were coached by the waterman Bob Coombes, who instructed his crew to take the inside arch under Hammersmith bridge. Oxford, a technically excellent crew, were coached by Thomas Egan, the Cambridge amateur coach who had offered his services to Oxford because of the Cambridge employment of Coombes. Oxford took the traditional centre arch. Cambridge lost the stream and a considerable margin by this manoeuvre, and lost the race by six lengths.

Egan of Caius and Arthur Shadwell of Balliol exerted a great influence on university rowing. They developed the longer smooth stroke used by early amateurs as opposed to the short choppy stroke of the professional watermen.

Racing was still undertaken in cutters and gigs with fixed seats. Limited sliding was sometimes achieved by oarsmen greasing the seats of their trousers or the use of sheepskin covers on the seats. The oars had heavy squared shafts and narrow blades, some only about two inches wide, which could break very easily. There was no button to hold them in the rowlocks, which consisted of two thole-pins projecting from the gunwale. These were subsequently incorporated into the structure of the boat itself for greater strength. The value of long leverage on the oars was recognised early, and the boats were broad in beam to allow the oarsmen to sit on the opposite side of the boat to their rowlocks and reach past the man in front at the start of the stroke. In 1846 the introduction of outriggers allowed boats to become much narrower.

The twelfth and final race of this irregular period took place in April 1854 and again resulted in a win for Oxford. Of the twelve races thus far, Cambridge had won seven and Oxford five.

1 *Map of the Putney to Mortlake course with photographs by Henry Taunt, 1887*

2 *The start from the Old Aqueduct, Putney, 1858, watercolour by Cambridge's number four, D Darroch*

Bridging the course

- *1729 Old Putney bridge (downstream of start)*
- *1827 Hammersmith chain bridge*
- *1849 Barnes railway bridge*
- *1855 Putney aqueduct*
- *1884 New Putney Bridge (widened 1931-33)*
- *1887 New Hammersmith bridge*
- *1889 Putney Railway bridge*
- *1933 Chiswick bridge (upstream of Finish)*

An Oxford boat with a Cornish accent   continued

The overall length and beam would be much the same as that of Davies, so why was his boat so well regarded at the time? First, she was light, being built of Quebec yellow pine (pinus strobus). The replica boats which I built in 2003 weigh a mere 400lb (180kg), and possibly in consequence had an advantage over a boat built of heavier timber. The Oxford gig, like most gigs, has a fairly flat and full bottom. This makes it much more stable but slower than a fine bilged boat. If you compare the Oxford boat with the Royal Oak, a four-oared racing boat also on show at the River and Rowing Museum at Henley and which dates from around 1812, you will see that Royal Oak is much more v-shaped and therefore faster than the Oxford boat, but only if her crew can sit her. From experience of rowing the Royal Oak with experienced men, this is not easy, for while she is still much broader than a modern racing hull, you are sitting up much higher and have much longer and heavier oars. Therefore the second advantage Oxford may have had in the first race in 1829 was a stable boat allowing a strong, enthusiastic crew to pull ahead. To put it another way, Cambridge may not have been able to sit their finer-lined boat.

Jackson's Oxford Journal described the boats in the 1829 race this way:
'We forgot to mention the manifest difference in the boats. The Cambridge boat, though London-built and launched new for the occasion and much gayer in appearance than the old Oxford boat, was far inferior in the water, dipping to the oar whilst the other rose to every stroke in fine style; and though the Oxford crew were stronger, the Cambridge might have given them more trouble if they had been equally well boated.'

24 BATTLE OF THE BLUES

One day was so cold that the spray was frozen all over my oar except the two spaces where my hands had thawed it. The next, horses were provided for the whole crew and we galloped over Richmond Park, a joy as real as it was unexpected.

Theodore Cook, Oxford 1889

1 *Cambridge sink off Barnes, 1978*

2 *Cambridge sink off Harrods, 1912*

3 *Oxford (foreground) sink at Putney, 1951*

4 *Bert Green, Oxford's Putney waterman, drives coach Steve Royle*

Weather plays a merry dance   DANIEL TOPOLSKI

The outcome of the boat race has often been crucially, and sometimes cruelly, decided by the weather. Wind, the strength of the tide, the toss for stations and a cox's split-second mid-race decision can win or lose the Battle of the Blues and coaches ignore the vagaries and powerful impact of these imponderables at their peril.

In theory the bends in the course cancel each other out, which ensures that both crews cover the same distance as long as they steer precisely parallel courses. The first bend at Fulham football ground favours the Middlesex crew by approximately a quarter of a length, the next big bend at Hammersmith gives a significant tactical advantage to Surrey of three quarters of a length with a further quarter length added on the bend at the top of Chiswick eyot before the Crossing. The advantage then transfers back to Middlesex, and from the Bandstand to the finish is worth three quarters of a length. In practise, effective coxing, tactical interpretation of the course by the coaches and weather conditions can profoundly affect the significance of these corners.

In a boat race, suffused as it is by bends, changing wind conditions, an elusive 'fastest stream' line and tidal strengths, there is usually one moment – or possibly two – when the race is won or lost. If a crew can collectively recognise that critical window of opportunity – a stroke, a position on the course, or a breakaway chance – the victory is theirs. In the days preceding the race it is the duty of the coaches to help the crew, and the cox in particular, to anticipate when those unpredictable fleeting moments could occur. But they can happen at any time and the weather conditions often play a crucial role.

BATTLE OF THE BLUES   25

1830 to 1855

Near Barnes Bridge by Gustave Doré, 1870

OTHER SKIRMISHES

Six eight-oared races took place between representative Oxford and Cambridge crews in the 1840s and 1850s, when there were no official boat races and therefore no awarding of blues. One was over the championship course in the Gold Cup event of the Thames Regatta in 1844, won by Oxford by four lengths. Leander, who were also in the race, came in third, some ten lengths adrift.

The other five races were all in the final of the Grand Challenge Cup at Henley regatta, over one mile 550 yards, about one-third of the length of the championship course. The first was in 1845 and was won by Cambridge by 'about two lengths'. The next was in 1847 and on this occasion the race went to Oxford by two lengths. There was then a gap until 1851 and this time Oxford won 'easily'. The fourth race, in 1853 was the only one in which there was a close finish. With a fresh north-east breeze blowing, Oxford 'won the toss' according to an early account and chose the Berks station. Cambridge took an early lead of 'the length of the bow', but Oxford, favoured by the station, then moved up on them. It is reported that the Cambridge four man unshipped his blade for a stroke or two by accident, but whether or not this influenced the result, Oxford won on the post by 'no more than 18 inches'.

Cambridge then won the 1855 race by two and a half lengths, giving them two wins to Oxford's four in these races.

Discipline involves in itself the notion of principles, and these, when carried into practice, enter into men's ways of thinking and feeling, and give a decided bias to their conduct as rowing men. Thus, like any constitutional maxims, they are much more than written law; they are not letter but spirit; and become the hereditary guides of every successive set of men in the boat club, a wholesome pervading system of tradition and a standard to which each man endeavours to act up. Discipline, in truth, has an immense moral effect, and that an enduring one.

A T W Shadwell
in Principles of Rowing, 1846

Weather plays a merry dance *continued*

There are few rules of engagement in the boat race, the most important being that both crews must go through the centre arch of Hammersmith and Barnes bridges whatever the water conditions. Furthermore, once a crew has established an open water lead, the cox may choose his course, which includes being allowed to move across in front of the trailing crew to secure the advantageous inside of subsequent bends. But he has to give way and move back to his station to avoid causing a foul by clashing (and inviting disqualification) should the trailing crew manage to restore an overlap; in practise, though, this rarely happens. If a crew sinks in rough conditions before the end of the Fulham wall, two and a half minutes from the start of the race, the umpire can order a re-row.

It is a given dictum that if the prevailing wind at Putney is a headwind for the crews, blowing from the north-west, it will be a rough first six minutes but that as the race passes under Hammersmith bridge and onto the big Surrey bend the ensuing two miles will flatten out as the wind becomes tail. Conversely the opposite conditions will apply when the wind is blowing hard from the south or southwest.

Crucially Hammersmith bridge provides the moment of change in wind direction and coaches have to factor this into their race plan to take account of the effect it will have on the speed of the boat, the predicted water conditions and the projected performance of the athletes. The Boat Race course provides one of the greatest challenges in rowing, and indeed in sport generally, precisely because its twisting four and a quarter mile course produces the sort of constantly changing conditions that no straight 2000 metre international race course would ever experience.

OXFORD TAKE THE LEAD

By 1855 there had been 12 races, for which the score was Cambridge seven, Oxford five and the course for the race had been established between Putney and Mortlake, though not always in that direction or with the same start and finish. The year 1856 saw the establishment of the annual event and began a period in which Oxford took over the overall lead in the series.

The 1856 race was from Mortlake to Putney on the ebb tide, the second occasion on which this direction was used, despite the advantage which it gave to the crew on the Middlesex station. This time the start was at 'Barker's rails', thought to have been about three minutes' rowing (i.e. about 1000 yards) upriver of The Ship. The start, like many in this period, was dramatic because the Cambridge number six Joseph M'Cormick caught a crab and cascaded backwards, causing the light blues to lose about a length. However, aided by their Middlesex station, they pulled up rapidly and were about half a length ahead by Barnes bridge. This was not the end of their misadventures. Two barges were in the way along Corney reach, and it was only by the quick reaction of the coxswains that neither crew hit them. The two crews remained very much in contention over the whole course and Cambridge won by a margin of only a half a length.

The race of 1857 was notable as the first in which a carvel-built keelless boat was used. This was built for Oxford by Matthew Taylor of Newcastle and rigged to the pattern in the north of England with stroke rowing on bow side. It was also the first race in which Edmond Warre rowed for Oxford. He was to exert a profound influence on Oxford rowing over some 50 years, particularly in his capacities of assistant master, headmaster and finally provost of Eton College. The race was an easy win for Oxford.

A crab again interfered with the start in 1858, this time by the Oxford stroke, but with greater damage, for his rigger was badly distorted. Though Cambridge went into the lead as a consequence, they did not have it all to their benefit, for they hit a moored barge on their way to victory by 22 seconds. The 1859 race was rowed in a northerly gale. Oxford won the toss and naturally chose Middlesex. Cambridge asked for a postponement but were refused. They kept their rivals waiting for about half an hour on station, but the wind did not abate. Cambridge, in the rougher conditions, gradually filled with water as they struggled up the course and became the first boat race sinking casualty between Barnes bridge and the finish. Inconvenient tide times meant that the 1860 race was rowed in the early morning. Interruptions by steamers delayed the start, and the race was eventually rowed at the turn of a very slack tide. Cambridge won, but in the slowest championship course time of 26 mins 5 secs.

BATTLE OF THE BLUES

1 *The Dead Heat, 1877, lithograph by Charles Robinson. Oxford are, curiously, depicted in light blue and Cambridge in pink.*

2 *Portraits of the crews, 1877*

3 *The 1877 finishing judge, Honest John Phelps, 'Dead-heat to Oxford by five feet'*

There should be no running before breakfast. I repeat, no running before breakfast!

I have very little doubt but that overtraining, and many of its concomitant evils, are caused by too much running rather than rowing.

Argonaut (E D Brickwood) in The Arts of Rowing and Training, 1866

Weather plays a merry dance continued

The skill and flexibility required to cope with these destabilising effects, coupled with the intense endurance demands made on the young non-professional athletes, helps to explain why the boat race retains such mystique and elicits the admiration of so wide and non-specialist an audience.

Coaches have always steered clear of showing a preference for one station or the other, because losing the toss and getting the 'wrong' side could undermine the confidence of their crew. But they have to prepare their athletes well in advance for the different tactics required by each station. The choice for the winner of the toss is determined more by the wind and tide conditions than the perceived strengths and weaknesses of the crew.

A strong headwind and rough water along the mile post reach would offer the Middlesex crew protection to the first bend for longer than it would the crew on Surrey. But to gamble on a crew being able to secure a clear water lead before the start of the Hammersmith bend has become increasingly unlikely as professional coaches have ensured that the crews are now more evenly matched than ever before.

It is still usually the case that, barring a choice of Middlesex made on the basis of weather conditions, Surrey provides the helpful cushion of a decisive advantage around Hammersmith at the six minute point where the crews could be feeling vulnerable. But today's crews are trained to race all the way over the four and a quarter mile track.

1856 to 1883

In the early 1860s there was still considerable interference with the races, both from normal river traffic and the numerous steamers following the race. In 1864, when the race was scheduled from Mortlake to Putney on the ebb tide, the two presidents attempted to control steamers by threatening to postpone the race if any steamers were in front of the crews at the start. With an ebb tide, the steamers would have been marooned on the Thames mud. Unfortunately the presidents could not carry out their threat because the Prince of Wales, who was following the race, had an urgent appointment shortly afterwards. However, in 1870 the steamer problem was substantially curtailed when the Thames Conservancy limited the number of following steamers to two.

Oxford moved into the ascendancy and won every race for nine years from 1861 to 1869. In 1864, after 21 races, the last four won easily, they took the lead in the series, which they were destined to retain for over 60 years.

There appear to be two main reasons for this superiority. The first was the presence of George Morrison, initially as oarsman, then as non-rowing president and subsequently and most importantly as leading coach in six of the nine Oxford-winning years. Warre, Walter 'Guts' Woodgate and George's younger brother, Allan, also played a part in the coaching team. Secondly, Cambridge's rowing technique declined when Tom Egan stopped coaching them in 1861, though whether this was causal or coincidental is conjecture. In 1869 and 1870 George Morrison came to coach Cambridge and was credited with the change in the light blue fortunes. This coincided with John Goldie joining the Cambridge crew, which gives an alternative explanation for their improvement.

Within these nine races, 1863 saw the third and last ebb tide row, starting from Barker's rails again, with Oxford winning from the Middlesex station. The 1866 race was notable for the watermanship of the Oxford coxswain, Charles Tottenham, when faced with an apparently inevitable crash with a barge which had swung across the river just below Barnes bridge. Tottenham managed to scrape under the stern, avoiding the clash by a matter of inches.

The Cambridge coxswain Arthur Forbes tangled with a barge in 1867 but not as effectively as Tottenham, for to avoid a clash with the bows he had to make such a violent correction that he lost something like three lengths. 1868 was tragic for Cambridge when one of their very promising blues from 1867, the Hon James Gordon, accidentally shot and killed himself while cleaning a rifle. When Oxford took the lead, Cambridge completely lost their cohesion.

1 Oxford versus Harvard in coxed fours, 1869. The start at Putney (top) and the finish at Mortlake, Oxford winning by about three and a half lengths in 22 mins 20 secs

2 Oxford's crew against Harvard, 1869. Bow F Willan, A C Yarborough, J C Tinné, stroke S D Darbishire, cox F H Hall

> In 1883 I coached both crews an equal number of days, and one day took Cambridge on a morning tideway course, and caught the train to Taplow in time for Oxford's afternoon show.
>
> Two-way 'Guts' Woodgate

Weather plays a merry dance *continued*

Crews have lost the race by sinking in five of the previous 149 races, most recently in 1978 when a waterlogged Cambridge failed to make the turn after Barnes bridge. An hour before the race, not content to guess at the likely head wind conditions at the crossing where both crews have to move across from Surrey towards Middlesex above Chiswick eyot, I had taken a ride with Bert Green, Oxford's launch driver and expert tideway adviser, up river to check the potential for sinking white horses for ourselves. Fellow coach Hugh Matheson, returning from an uncomfortable sculling session, confirmed our concerns. As a consequence we strengthened the splashboards and waterbreak we had already attached to the boat in the minutes before the crews went afloat. Cambridge took minimal precautions, did not fit splashboards, and sank.

Since the first boat race crew I coached in 1973 filled with water in the opening minutes of the race and lost by 13 lengths, I have kept a photograph of their half submerged despair as they struggled bravely but vainly, still rating 35, under Hammersmith bridge, to remind me never to underestimate the powers of the tideway in a belligerent mood. While battery-operated pumps are often used to expel water that has washed into the boat, preventing it coming in in the first place was always my preferred option. Inflated inner tubes under the seats to take up space, broad splashboards along the sides of the boat, a big breakwater behind the bowman and aerofoil riggers, designed specially by the great innovative Oxford coach Jumbo Edwards to cut through the waves rather than create a block to them, were devices we employed to ensure the crew stayed on top of the water.

Hammersmith Bridge on Boat Race day, 1870s

Morrison came to Cambridge for a short time in 1869 and for longer in 1870, and with Goldie as president and stroke there began a golden period in Cambridge rowing history. Goldie stroked also in 1871 and 1872, and Cambridge prevailed in all three races. In 1872 it subsequently emerged that Goldie had broken a bolt in his rigger in Crabtree reach and could therefore only set the stroke without doing any work. Goldie is honoured by the naming of the Cambridge boathouse.

Sliding seats, developed by John Clasper, a professional oarsman and boatbuilder who had moved from Newcastle to the tideway, were used by both crews in 1873. Cambridge adapted to these rapidly and won in 1873 and 1874, but in 1875 Oxford won by 10 lengths. Cambridge followed that by a win in 1876 described as 'easily'.

In 1877 the only dead-heat occurred, and given the technical help available by the 21st century, it is unlikely to be repeated. Doubts have been expressed over the years about the probity of the waterman, 'Honest John' Phelps, who acted as regular finish judge. He is reputed to have declared it as a 'Dead-heat to Oxford by five feet' ('yards' in some accounts), a decision which was subsequently recorded by umpire Joseph Chitty as 'dead-heat'. It is, however, important to appreciate that in 1877 there was no defined finish line and that the crush of craft around the finish was such that the skiff of the judge may well have been substantially displaced from its proper position.

Weather plays a merry dance *continued*

Sinking is the most dramatic outcome of a failure to take account of the wind. Less obvious are the tactical decisions made to deal with difficult wind conditions which can determine the outcome of the race – decisions like the cox cutting a corner in mid-race because of a slack tide, or getting out of the fastest but roughest stream to give his crew a smoother ride, or the coaches making a pre-race assessment. Oxford's decision to make for the Middlesex shore at the start of the 1987 race was decisive because it drew Cambridge over from the Surrey station to join them, a manoeuvre that required them to cover extra unnecessary distance.

In practical terms a strong tide pushes the fastest water out wider around the bends while a slack tide encourages the coxes to steer a tighter course and cut the corners. Evaluating the strength and likely effect of the tide is vital, especially when strong winds create a rough chop on exposed stretches of the course. Knowing when, or if, to seek shelter from a headwind at a significant point in the race can make the difference between victory and defeat. But moving out of the fastest tide to avoid the worst of the rough water can be costly, because it allows a crew that has confidence to hold its form in the fastest but roughest stream to make considerable gains.

Scheduling regular visits to train on, and acclimatise to, the tideway through the winter is of enormous benefit to a boat race squad, and racing fixtures against local clubs over the course provide essential familiarity with its unique and unpredictable waters. To this end Oxford always held its two-week January training camp at Putney during the seventies and eighties and visited the tideway every second weekend. Failing to respect this essential homework, by limiting the tideway experience, puts a crew (and particularly a cox) at a serious disadvantage.

As little mental and sedentary work as possible should be undertaken; and, where practicable, as much spare time as can be allowed should be devoted to the amusement of mind, by walks and horse-exercise, witnessing cricket and other out-doors sports – but standing about too long is to be avoided – and by occasional participation in a game of billiards, or other in-door diversions.

The Arts of Rowing and Training, 1866

At Barnes Bridge in 1870

In 1878 the finish was marked by a post and Edward Fairrie, who had rowed for Cambridge in 1856, took over the duty of finish judge. Since that year the job has always been fulfilled by a previous blue. The 1878 race gave the finish judge no difficulties, for Oxford were a much stronger crew and won by 40 seconds. The standard of rowing at both universities in 1879 was down on that which had been seen in recent years, but Cambridge won comfortably.

There then followed a series of four Oxford wins from from 1880 to 1883. The race of 1880 was notable for being the only one which has been postponed from Saturday to Monday due to thick fog. In 1881, the dark blue victory was achieved despite their number six, David Brown, being taken ill on the morning of the race.

The 1883 race was a fiasco from the start. From 1840, or possibly earlier, the race had been started by Edward Searle seated in a skiff between the crews. The practice was for him to warn the crews of the starting procedure, ask 'Are you ready?' and drop a white handkerchief while saying 'Go'. By 1883 he was old and his voice was feeble. Neither crew heard the order 'Go'. Leonard West (stroke of Oxford) saw the handkerchief fall and moved away, Frederick Meyrick (Cambridge) stayed put, expecting a recall. Oxford temporarily halted, then realising that the umpire was not going to make a recall, rowed on and left their rivals in confusion. After this Searle was relieved of his post and from then on the race was started by the umpire, initially with a pistol.

Of the 28 races from 1856 to 1883, Oxford won 17, Cambridge 10, and there was one dead-heat. Oxford were ahead 22 to 17 in the series.

Every quarter of an hour in bed before twelve o'clock is equal to an inch of water before the rowlock.

Maxim quoted in The Arts of Rowing and Training, 1866

Weather plays a merry dance   *continued*

What is apparent though is that there is little difference between the two coaching teams in their perception of the best and fastest route from Putney to Mortlake. The challenge is to give the coxes confidence to follow that best pathway, to recognise instinctively the vital guiding landmarks, to understand the marker points signifying where to begin and end their negotiation of the bends, how to avoid getting across the tide and to acknowledge that gentle but constant use of the rudder will coax a boat along the course far more effectively than heavy-handed steering. In the words of Bert Green, 'the boat will steer itself if you'll only let it'.

Clashing is usually caused inadvertently by a cox looking across at, and steering off, his rival rather than at the river ahead, or by taking a turn too late or too early. In the battle to secure the fastest stream for their crew, the coxes often veer too closely together and overlap the oars. The resultant clash, or at least the unhelpful weaving back and forth caused by violent steering, has a detrimental destabilising effect on boat speed as well as on the focus of the athletes working at the peak of their effort.

To reduce the potential for problems during the race the university boat clubs have recently established a panel of umpires which monitors, advises, trains and regulates their performances in fixtures and races. The two coxing advisers as well as the coxes now go over the course with the umpire before the race so that everyone involved understands the inherent difficulties and any differences there may be in interpreting the rules and the umpire's instructions. But whatever is done to try to minimise the unforeseen, nature's unpredictable forces, the wind and the tide, will invariably guarantee that something dramatic turns up to confound the experts.

BOSPOROS

36   BATTLE OF THE BLUES

Hatred is what you need.
Contempt implies complacency.

Dan Topolski, Oxford coach 1993

1   *Stanley Muttlebury coaching Cambridge, 1892*

2   *Daniel Topolski coaching Oxford, 1982*

3   *Oxford coached from horseback on the Isis, 1913*

How to peak on the right day   DONALD LEGGET

Coaching of the university boat race crews was until recently the preserve of former blues or Oxbridge oarsmen, who freely and willingly gave up weeks of holidays or of their time. All the coaching was done on an amateur basis. Until the 1970s, university rowing did not become really serious until January. Nowadays both university squads form as early as September, having been training most of the year.

Before professional coaches were introduced, each president used to invite his own team of coaches. It was as autocratic as that. They would meet on Saturdays to discuss the week's progress and whittle down the numbers of trialists. In the Lent term leading up to the race itself, there would be five or six coaches each doing a two-week period, with the final three weeks coached by a 'finishing' coach. In 1973 Oxford were finished by Dan Topolski who, though Oxford lost that year, set up a system which was responsible for Oxford winning 17 of 19 races between 1974 and 1992.

Coaching a boat race crew is not easy. One starts with a bunch of oarsmen who used to number well over fifty, but now is nearer twenty-five, and whittle it down to sixteen. In the early days there were no ergometers or seat races to sort out the wheat from the chaff. Selection was done largely by eye, reliance on reputation prior to Oxbridge, or on small boat racing at each university. Only on Saturdays did the coaches see the oarsmen in eights, rowing a lock-to-lock on the Isis or the Cam. A poor performance by a crew could sink someone's hopes. Richard Budgett suffered this fate at Cambridge, never getting into the blue boat before moving on to the University of London, where he won a world medal and then an Olympic gold in 1984.

FLOREAT ETONA

Oarsmen educated at Eton College have exerted a major influence on the boat race over the whole series. Thus of the 2682 competitors in the 149 races to 2003, just over a quarter have previously been educated at Eton College: for Cambridge, just over 20 per cent; for Oxford just under 31 per cent. In the period from 1884 to 1914, however, just over 34 per cent of Cambridge competitors were from Eton, and for Oxford an astounding 60 per cent. During this period Eton were undoubtedly the best rowing school as judged by their results at Henley, and Oxford benefited from this.

During the six years 1884 to 1889, Oxford won only one race, in 1885. This was largely due to the fact that Frederick Pitman, the only member of this important rowing family to come to Cambridge, was selected as stroke in 1884 and proved to be outstanding. The 1884 race was won easily by Cambridge, but the 1885 race was regarded as an even greater triumph for Pitman even though Cambridge lost it. They came to the start conceding almost eight pounds per man and with a late substitute for their number six, J C Brown, who broke a rib during the final week. At Hammersmith Oxford were up by five seconds but just after this they lurched badly due to Percy Taylor, their number three, dislocating his shoulder (and re-locating it). Oxford got together again and were leading by thirteen seconds at Chiswick church and twelve at Barnes bridge. Pitman then raised the Cambridge rate to 41 and, ably supported by his crew, held it at that rate until they were overlapping their rivals. They had no more to give and Oxford went away to win by eight seconds.

Pitman's third race in 1886 was just as exciting. Hammersmith bridge was being repaired and there was only just enough space for two crews to get through together. Arrangements were made for a restart if there was an accidental clash under the bridge. In the event both crews went through level without touching. Oxford then went into the lead and, on Surrey, were six seconds ahead at Barnes bridge. Pitman then put in a similar spurt to the previous year and this time won by two seconds. This was the first boat race in which a crew behind at Barnes won the race.

Photolithographs by Dawson

1 *Towards the finish seen from the Surrey shore, 1896*

2 *Passing Chiswick Steps seen from the Surrey shore, 1890*

3 *Emerging from Barnes Bridge seen from the Middlesex shore, 1891*

4 *Punch cartoon, 1954*

Recipe for jelly

Take two calves-feet and two quarts of water; boil to one quart; stand till cold; take off the oil. Take the juice and rind of two lemons, the whites of two eggs, six oz of sugar, and whip them together; put to boil for five minutes; set aside for 15 minutes; then pass through a bag. Add half pint of sherry and one wineglass of brandy.

1870s

How to peak on the right day *continued*

The boat race is held at the end of most oarsmen's winter training, prior to racing at regattas in the summer. Oxford and Cambridge therefore have half the usual amount of time afforded to most clubs and universities to get themselves up to a peak for one vital race where the winner takes all. The intake varies hugely from seasoned international and university oarsmen from abroad, to promising schoolboys, to virtual novices who have come up through the college clubs at Oxford or Cambridge. Cambridge's vastly better system of college rowing and coaching underpinned their boat race crews in the 1900s.

A boat race coach could find himself coaching an Olympic medallist alongside a couple of novices. It is the skill in being able to weld the strengths and weaknesses together over a two-week period that marks out a good boat race coach. The measure of success in this at Cambridge used to be a 'certificate' from Alf Twinn, CUBC's boatman for more than fifty years, delivered by the accolade 'they were all right when you left them'. For more than ten years I started the Cambridge crews in the first fortnight in January, so it wasn't difficult to earn that certificate, but come the 1980s training stretched back into October, making one's commitment even harder and the pain of losing even greater.

It was this commitment that eventually pushed both clubs into employing professional coaches. No longer could the programme be won on one session a day. Ergometers and land training in the early mornings four times a week is now the norm, followed by fifteen miles – now referred to as twenty to twenty-five kilometres – on the water.

BATTLE OF THE BLUES 39

In 1887 it looked as though Oxford might get their revenge. After Barnes, when Cambridge were ahead by eight seconds, Oxford were drawing up rapidly but the blade of the Oxford number seven, Hector McLean, snapped in two at the button, and Cambridge rowed on to win.

The last few years of the 1880s with Stanley Muttlebury in the crew was a brief good period of Cambridge rowing, for they won with ease in 1888 and with the same oarsmen won again in 1889, though not so easily. However, they were to pay for president Muttlebury's scant attention to the future when selecting his crews. In 1890 Oxford moved into one of their best periods of the nineteenth century, equalling their record of 1861-1869 by winning nine consecutive races again. In 1890 and 1891, there were well matched crews and very close races resulted, Oxford winning by one length in 1890 and half a length in 1891. The 1891 result was perhaps artificially close because although the dark blues had four outstanding oarsmen on board, namely Lord Ampthill (president), William 'Wal' Fletcher and the brothers Guy and Vivien Nickalls, they also had two men who had just recovered from influenza. The stroke of this crew, Charles Kent, became finish judge from 1928 to 1951.

1 *Putney to Mortlake depicted in The Graphic, 1870*

2 *'Oh! Well rowed…' Tumultuous crowd from Reminiscences of Oxford Varsity Life, c1880*

He infected me, as he infected all of us at Fieldhead, with the regularly recurrent leaping fever of excitement about the boat race. Every year we grew more and more tense as the day approached, listening as if our lives depended on it to the prognostications of the experts at the breakfast table. I really believe it was the most important day of the year for my father, a great spring festival and consulting of omens: if Cambridge won the crops would grow; if Oxford beat them, the future seemed dangerous and dark, only to be redeemed perhaps by the triumph of a Trinity or Leander crew at Henley later on.

John Lehmann on his father Rudie Lehmann, Cambridge coach.

How to peak on the right day *continued*

The challenges which face today's coaches are just as great as they ever were. Every year there will be nine or ten guys trying their utmost to be in the top eight. Sometimes such pressures force a crew to peak too early. At other times, the last-minute sudden surge of speed makes nonsense of the form book, no more so than in the famous mutiny race of 1987, when an Oxford crew surrounded by weeks of acrimony and dispute and without several of its star oarsmen beat a Cambridge boat expected by most pundits to carry it off.

The 2003 race was the closest ever, and no crew had ever overcome such a weight disadvantage to win as Oxford did that day. History will forget that Cambridge lost their bow man two days before the race, but the oarsmen and the coaches never will.

It is sobering to note that nine of the twenty oarsmen and coxes in Great Britain's open world championship team in 2003 had competed in the boat race plus two of the Canadian team and one Dutchman. Faced with that, who can stand up and say that the boat race is an anachronism? Its oarsmen and their coaches make an enormous contribution to the sport of rowing.

BATTLE OF THE BLUES   41

1 2

42 BATTLE OF THE BLUES

…It then seemed that Oxford were coming over further than they ought, so I warned Oxford. As the words escaped my mouth I noticed the Cambridge bow man losing his blade, the Cambridge crew ground to a halt, the blade over his head and stuck under the boat, whatever. When that happens you have to slow down quite a lot otherwise you can't get it back, which is what happened. Oxford got a significant advantage out of that.

Rupert Obholzer, umpire 2001

The umpire takes charge   MIKE SWEENEY

The first boat race, held in Henley in 1829, had three officials – an Oxford umpire, a Cambridge umpire and a referee. During the early years of the race umpiring was sometimes carried out on horseback. A pistol was used to start the race rather than the dropping of a flag, and the coxing of the crews was undertaken by professional watermen who regarded fouls as a part of the game. All in all, this was an interesting mixture for an embryo boat race umpire endeavouring to ply his trade.

By the latter half of the 1900s the role and operation of the umpire had settled into a pattern. The choice of the umpire each year was a joint arrangement between the two clubs. In an even year Cambridge would offer the names of three Cambridge men to Oxford, who would then choose between them. In an odd year the procedure was reversed, Oxford putting forward three men and Cambridge making the choice.

In the run up to the race, the chosen umpire would try to visit each crew at their training venue, to start to get to know them as individuals. He would then join each crew for one or more outings on the tideway in the week before the race, one session to include practice starts from a stakeboat. On the day, the umpire would start the race and officiate from aboard the official launch of the other university.

In most years this procedure worked reasonably well, but occasionally it fell down! One year, one of the universities tried to 'force' their opponents to accept their particular choice for umpire by listing his name along with two other candidates who were both very senior blues and very out of touch with rowing. Needless to say, the other university refused to be hustled and chose one of the two senior men. The plot thickened when the chosen umpire, being unsure of the line of the tide around the Fulham bend, took advice from the coaches and old blues travelling with him in the other university's launch!

1884 to 1914

In 1892 Charles Pitman, brother of Frederick who had stroked Cambridge in the mid-1880s, came up to Oxford and stroked them for three of the next four years (in 1893 he rowed seven). The 1893 Oxford crew was the first to complete the course in under 19 minutes (18 mins 45 secs) and held the record until 1911. Pitman was in four successful Oxford crews and when he went down in 1895, he was succeeded by Harcourt Gold as stroke, and Oxford's winning streak continued. The 1896 race was notable for very rough water from Hammersmith onwards. Gold tucked in behind the Cambridge crew in the shelter of the Surrey shore and Oxford were still just behind at Barnes bridge, though now on the Middlesex shore and keeping their rivals out in the rougher water. In the final reach Gold pulled up and passed Cambridge to win by one second, the closest winning margin in the race thus far.

During this winning period, although Cambridge often had competent crews, including such famous oarsmen as Muttlebury, Charles Fogg-Elliot, Raymond Etherington-Smith and Claude Goldie (son of John), the dark blues had a succession of brilliant oarsmen of whom many won four races. This was the period of cartoon portraits by Spy, the nom de plume of Sir Leslie Ward, who commemorated many oarsmen from both universities in Vanity Fair.

As already noted, the Oxford link with Eton College rowing was very strong over this period. From 1890 to 1898, 70 per cent of the Oxford oarsmen came from Eton. Eton's coaching was in the hands of the headmaster, the great Edmond Warre, assisted by Reginald de Havilland (Oxford president in 1884), who coached eleven Eton crews to win the Ladies' Plate at Henley. It might perhaps be said that at this time 'the boat race was won on the Thames at Eton'. Nor was the coaching at Oxford itself deficient, for during the 1890s regular coaches included Fletcher, Gilbert Bourne, Douglas McLean, and Rudie Lehmann, a formidable stable.

Light Blue heavies

1 *John Goldie (Cambridge 1869 to 1872) gave his name to the boathouse on the Cam and the reserve crew*

2a *Banner Johnstone (Cambridge 1904 to 1906 and against Harvard, 1906) became a successful coach and rowing correspondent*

2b *Rudie Lehmann, founder of Granta magazine, coached Oxford, Cambridge and Harvard, and Cambridge to success against Harvard in 1906*

2c *Duggie Stuart (Cambridge 1906 to 1909 and against Harvard, 1906) was criticised for a style named after him that he did not beget*

2d *Stanley Muttlebury (Cambridge 1886 to 1890) picked the same crew for two years when president, and went on to be a successful coach*

2a - 2d *Illustrations by Spy (Sir Leslie Ward) from Vanity Fair*

44 BATTLE OF THE BLUES

Everyone, the whole of London, the costermongers, the drivers of four-wheelers, those delicious Hansom cabs – the gondolas of London as Disraeli called them – everyone cared about the Boat Race. All wore the colours, light blue or dark blue. In the household everyone, the housemaid, the butler, there were great divisions. My father was at Cambridge, so as a child we were Cambridge. Nannie was violently for Oxford. And on the day, on that great day, the whole of London, people in offices, streets and homes, cared only for this great event.

Harold Macmillan, former prime minister and chancellor of Oxford University, 1979

The umpire takes charge *continued*

No major event ever stands still, even one as traditional as the boat race. Thus, in 1981, Ronnie Howard (Oxford) insisted on a break with tradition by umpiring the race that year from his own, completely neutral, launch. The umpire's splendid isolation did not last long, as a BBC TV cameraman and a sound technician joined Ronnie and subsequent umpires.

By 1983 Howard had become almost a fixture as the Oxford umpire, officiating in 1973, 1977, 1979, 1981 and 1983. When I was asked to officiate at the 1984 race I immediately contacted Ronnie to glean as much experience from him as possible about the handling of this unique event. There was very little written down to assist a new umpire, with the exception of Ronnie's definitive description of the two different ways that the clubs prepared for the start commands – blades squared on the 'Are you ready?' or blades flat on the water on the 'Are you ready?' One of his less comforting bits of advice was 'don't wear Wellington boots – they are difficult to swim in!'

As it happened, regardless of my experience as a fully qualified international umpire, nothing could have prepared me for the events of the 1984 boat race. History records that Cambridge managed to hit a moored barge before the start of the race. They sank, they were rescued, a heavy debate then ensued as to what time and when to hold the race, which resulted in the first Sunday boat race of the century. My view of umpiring this extraordinary annual event was changed for ever. In each of my ensuing encounters with the two universities I became increasingly aware of just how many exceptional and unexpected scenarios were possible – fraught is an inadequate description!

Oxford trialists for the 1913 Boat Race pose with their coaches

In 1898 the Cambridge president William Dudley-Ward recognised that the technique at Cambridge was poor and, despite considerable opposition, invited Fletcher to come over from Oxford to help with the coaching. Although the light blues lost in 1899, they won the next year, helped also by Lehmann, who also came over from Oxford. This prevented Gold from winning his fourth race.

In 1900 Cambridge boated a very strong crew and Oxford a weak one, and the light blues won by 20 lengths, equalling the then record time of 18 mins 45 secs. Cambridge then had a period of relative strength, winning eight out of ten encounters between 1899 and 1908. The 1901 race, one of those won by the dark blues, was similar in many respects to that of 1896, with Oxford tucking in behind their rivals along the Surrey shore in rough conditions and then winning from the Middlesex station by one second, having been behind at Barnes bridge.

Cambridge won the next three races easily but that of 1903, the first to be umpired by Frederick Pitman, was a fiasco. The starting pistol stuck at half cock. The inexperienced Pitman failed to see that Cambridge had been dragged off the stakeboat by the tide, so that when the pistol eventually fired they had a start of between a quarter and half a length. Oxford were so dismayed that their rowing went completely to pieces. The 1904 race was the only one in which neither president could row, due to injuries.

The umpire takes charge *continued*

To give a few examples of the umpire's lot, in 1987 the race started in a storm, the umpire's launch lost steerage before the start, and the umpire, Colin Moynihan (Oxford), was transferred into one of the large launches, being nearly strangled en route as he was still attached to the throat microphone in the original launch. He started the race with the red flag and then discovered that the white flag (for warning the crews during the race) had been left behind in the original launch.

In 1990, in the Isis-Goldie race, John Garrett (Cambridge) became the first umpire of the century to disqualify one of the crews. He disqualified Isis after a collision just before Barnes bridge which left one of the Goldie crew with a broken gate. His decision was on the grounds that Isis had caused the clash and that Goldie could not row on. In 1997 Tom Cadoux-Hudson (Oxford) issued over 100 warnings to the two crews between the start and Chiswick steps. His vocal chords must have been severely stressed by the time that the race finished at Mortlake.

The issue of coxes being slow to respond to repeated verbal warnings, or even ignoring the umpire and aggressively continuing to push the other crew, appears to have been on an upward spiral in recent years. In 2001 Rupert Obholzer (Oxford) was faced with a clash of blades on the Fulham bend that left the Cambridge bow man without his oar. Rupert decided to stop the race and to restart the crews level. This was a highly publicised and much debated decision. The rules of the boat race are very clear when a clash occurs: 'The Umpire shall be the sole judge of a boat's proper course – in the event of a serious or deliberate foul the Umpire shall disqualify the offending crew.' The difficulty for the umpire is that both coxes will be pushing to be in the fastest part of the incoming tide or where they have been taught that the line of the tide runs. There are many different views on the correct line of the tide but, in the end, only the umpire's view is valid on the day. If coxes fail to respond to the umpire's warnings, especially when a serious clash occurs, they risk being disqualified.

Now sixteen youngsters in their pride of muscle

Prepare at Putney for the final tussle.

Two puny tyrants of the coxswain tribe

Whom threats deter not nor caresses bribe,

Hold in their hands, those ruthless hands, the fate,

Each, as he steers it, of his labouring eight.

Through the long weeks these men must meekly train,

Their style as pretty as their food is plain.

Primed with small beer and filled with prunes and rices,

They tempt each day the waves of Cam or Isis.

Eggs they may eat but not the tasty rasher

Who to Clayhithe proceed or to the Lasher,

And tarts and jams and entrees are taboo

To those who daily row in either crew.

R C Lehmann in Anni Fugaces, 1901

The 1905 race was won by Oxford with relative ease, and then Cambridge took the next three. These excited considerable controversy among the aficionados due to the unorthodox style of both crews. It was expected that the university crews would not only produce a fast row, but would demonstrate the ideal orthodox long stroke with good swing, quick catch and good draw through at the finish. The 1905 to 1908 crews used a short fast, jabbing stroke, shorter oars and little swing. It was attributed, perhaps unfairly, to Douglas Stuart, the Cambridge stroke, with the result that it was known by the derogatory title of 'Stuart's sculling style' but Oxford also tried it. Indeed some ascribe it to Wal Fletcher in coaching Christ Church Oxford, though this seems unlikely since he had been a coach of orthodoxy.

In 1908 the Oxford trial eights race set out to determine whether the orthodox or the 'Stuart' style was preferable, and orthodoxy won convincingly. There was further support from the performances of a Leander eight of veteran Oxford and Cambridge oarsmen rowing the traditional style in the 1908 Olympic regatta. The boat race this year was well contested, with Cambridge winning by two and a half lengths, but only after a tight race all the way to Barnes bridge.

The year 1909 saw not only the return of the orthodox style at both universities, but the first appearance of Robert Bourne, son of the great Dr G C Bourne, as stroke in the Oxford boat. Also available to Oxford were James Gillan and Collier Cudmore (both from the 1908 GB Olympic four) and Harold Barker, making a very competent crew. Bourne was to win not only this race by three and a half lengths but those of 1910 (also by three and a half lengths), 1911 (by two and three quarter lengths) and then 1912 by a magnificent six lengths. For the last two of these he was president. The first of these races was close until after Hammersmith, but the later ones were much easier victories.

From the historical viewpoint the 1911 and 1912 races were probably the most interesting. The 1911 race produced a record time of 18 mins 29 secs, which was to stand until 1934. It was followed in the Oxford launch by the Prince of Wales and his brother Prince Albert, and was the first race in which a number of aeroplanes flew over the competing crews.

1   Oxford in 1913: walking on the Embankment

2   Oxford in 1913: Prince of Wales on board Consuta

3   Oxford in 1913: Prince of Wales with president Wormald

4   Oxford in 1913: Disembarking after the race which Oxford won by three-quarters of a length

The umpire takes charge   *continued*

Fortunately, but as is the way with the two university boat clubs, this incident prompted several meetings to clear the air and to determine a better way for the future. From the umpire's point of view it was made very clear to both clubs that without the full and honest co-operation of the coaches and the coxes the umpire is not in a position to deliver a 'clean' race over this most difficult of courses. This point was accepted. The decision was then taken to create a boat race umpires' panel, consisting of four umpires from each university, chaired by a senior umpire, and tasked with sharing experience and pooling expertise amongst the team.

The umpires' panel has been up and running since the end of 2001. Now each year the umpire is supported by an assistant umpire in the launch (to deal with radio and telephone communications), an assistant umpire as the aligner on the start line, and other members of the panel check coxes' weights and safety features on the boats. There is also, of course, the umpire of the Isis-Goldie race. In 2003, at the panel's initiative, permanent, fixed anchors for the two stakeboats at the start have been set into the bed of the River Thames just upstream from Putney bridge. In addition, numerous 'exceptional scenarios' have been identified, listed, debated and their outcomes determined.

Who said nothing ever changes in the boat race!

Hammersmith Bridge on Boat Race Day, 1862, by Walter Greaves

Stage setting and management DUNCAN CLEGG

Superficially the organisational structure of the boat race has changed considerably in the first years of the 21st century, though the fundamentals remain the same. These are that the same dozen or so people provide the same services for the race year on year. If they have not been contacted by early January they are invariably on the telephone by mid January to ask anxiously, 'You do want me again this year, don't you?'

This is one of the joys of organising the race. It has a family feel – the Kents who have provided finishing judges for four generations, Chas Newens who provides half the launches (and a good deal else besides), Jim Cobb who organises the stakeboats, Jim Madden who is the police inspector at Putney – but a family who, though they have never themselves rowed in the race, are as passionate about it as anyone who ever has.

What brought about the change is the dramatically increased value of sponsorship over the most recent fifteen years and the consequent requirements of successive sponsors for more and more support from the race for their endeavours. In addition, since enduring the loss of many of its established sporting events in the late 1990s, BBC Television has rebuilt its competitive position and has become much more demanding in so doing.

Since the late 1980s, too, both clubs have moved to professional coaching, and so the club coaching and equipment establishments have increased in size and cost. As the race has no sources of income other than the sponsor and the BBC, it has become critical to the continued financial health and the success of the clubs to manage these relationships much more actively, with the result that the job of London Representative has become very much more time-consuming.

Nearly every servant lass declares herself by a bow in her cap. The budding juvenile coaxes a handkerchief of the colour he espouses out of his mother, and the dog at Hammersmith bridge marches about for days before the event with light blue round his neck and dark blue on his tail. Sundry bipeds did far worse than that at Mortlake. They were with Cambridge till the race was over, and then they whipped Oxford reserve ribbons out of their breast coat pockets.

Illustrated London News,
20 April 1867

In 1912 both crews sank (Cambridge just short of Harrods and Oxford just after the Doves), though Oxford managed to empty their boat and row on to the finish. Umpire Pitman declared the race void and ordered a re-row on the following Monday. The gale was even worse then, but had swung round to the north, and by agreement the stakeboats were moored close to the Fulham wall. Oxford won the toss, chose Middlesex and both crews crept round under the bank as far as Hammersmith, after which conditions were better. Oxford were already three lengths up at Hammersmith and pressed on to a six-length win.

Bourne went down after the 1912 race and Oxford supremacy was over, but they managed to win the 1913 race by dogged determination. They were behind right to Barnes bridge, where the deficit was four seconds, and on Middlesex they put in a fine drive, stroked by Ewart Horsfall, and won by three-quarters of a length. In 1914 Oxford never really settled down; for some strange reason they moved Horsfall to the four seat and Cambridge had an easy victory by four and a half lengths.

Of the 71 races to 1914, Oxford had won 39, Cambridge 31, with the one dead-heat. There were to be no more boat races until 1920 due to the 1914-18 world war, during which 42 blues lost their lives.

52 BATTLE OF THE BLUES

Puxley of Brasenose was known afterwards as 'Lot's Wife' because he looked round several times during the race and cheered us up enormously by shouting 'Now we are gaining!'

Theodore Cook in The Sunlit Hours

1 Easy win for Cambridge, 1906

2 The start from Putney Bridge, 2003

Stage setting and management *continued*

Whilst looking for a replacement sponsor for Beefeater Gin in 1999, we recognised that the job of London Representative had become too demanding to be done by one old blue volunteer any longer. I and my immediate predecessors, Alan Mays-Smith and Alan Burrough (who between us served the race for 45 years) took most decisions ourselves after consultation with the senior treasurers of the two university boat clubs. Since 2000, the London Representative has assumed the chair of P to M Ltd. This is the operating company, owned by the Oxford and Cambridge Rowing Foundation, which contracts with the clubs on the one hand and the sponsor and the BBC on the other to put the race on each year, and it is the board of P to M which now sets the policy for the race. In 2000 we also decided to appoint a professional to carry out the bulk of the day-to-day administration work, reporting to the London Representative and to the board.

So the tasks of producing the crews and now of organising the mechanics of the race is no longer in the hands of old blues as it was until ten years ago. This progression is, I think, inevitable and indeed vital for continuing the increase in the standards of the race, but is bound to have an impact, for however dedicated someone who has not rowed in the race may be, he will not see it in quite the same way as someone who has. This may be particularly true in regard to some of the more traditional aspects of the race, which may not have a direct impact on boat speed, but are important contributory elements to the public appeal.

For example, both crews have abandoned arriving at Putney on race day in their full regatta kit and now turn up in a scruffy mixture of training clothes, despite the preferences of both sponsor and public. Performance increases and traditions are not incompatible; it simply requires a modicum of thought and discipline by both clubs. The challenge is and will increasingly be to ensure that, while increasing the standards of performance, the underlying traditions and ethos are not altered without good reason, or the race damaged so that it loses this public appeal. For if the public following goes, so too does the television coverage, and if that happens the value to the sponsor diminishes dramatically.

LIGHT BLUES FIGHT BACK

In the 25 years before the 1914-1918 war, Cambridge won only nine boat races. In the twenty years from when the boat race re-started in 1920 to the start of the 1939-1945 war, Oxford won only three. The tide turned light blue in 1930 as Cambridge regained the lead they had lost in 1863, and they have not lost it since, although they came close to doing so in the 1980s.

Although crews from both universities took part in peace regattas in Henley and Paris in 1919, it was considered impractical to organise a boat race. The official boat race series started again with the 72nd race in the Easter vacation of 1920. Cambridge had the easier task in selecting their crew, with five of their 'peace' crew of 1919 available. One of these was Percival Hartley, who stroked three winning crews. There had been doubt whether public interest would revive, but the crowds along the towpath in 1920 were as large as ever. The 1920 race was uneventful, with Cambridge holding a modest lead until the Doves, when both crews encountered a strong headwind and rough water. Cambridge were on the Surrey station and ahead, and Oxford drew in behind them and tried to displace Cambridge from the inside line along Duke's Meadows, but the light blues had a comfortable margin and moved on to win by four lengths.

The light blues also won the 1921 and 1922 races, although their win in 1921 was only by one length after a tight race to Barnes bridge at which stage Oxford were in the lead by one second. The 1922 win was much more comfortable (four and a half lengths), although Cambridge's rowing style was criticised as it had been in pre-war days. It was suggested that university rowing was being influenced too much by the views of Steve Fairbairn, the Australian who had brought Jesus College to prominence before the war.

Oxford won by three quarters of a length in 1923 which turned out to be their last win for thirteen years. The Cambridge style was improving under the coaching of David Wauchope, and by 1924, when Francis Escombe joined the coaching team, orthodoxy prevailed again and the Cambridge winning margin was four and a half lengths. In 1926 Wauchope and Escombe were joined by William Dudley Ward, making a formidable coaching triumvirate, which was to stand the light blues in good stead for many years.

The year 1925 was a miserable one for Oxford. They had a lot of sickness during training and they were far from racing fitness when they came to the start. Their problems were further compounded by losing the toss with a 'sinking wind', a north-westerly gale in which the Surrey station is almost un-rowable. Their craft filled rapidly with water, held up at first by the air-filled bladders under the seats, but eventually sank off the Doves, leaving Cambridge to paddle on to victory. Frederick Pitman, the very experienced umpire, was criticised for not putting the stake-boats close to the Fulham wall, but with the balance between protection from the wind and getting less of the tide, this is always a difficult decision.

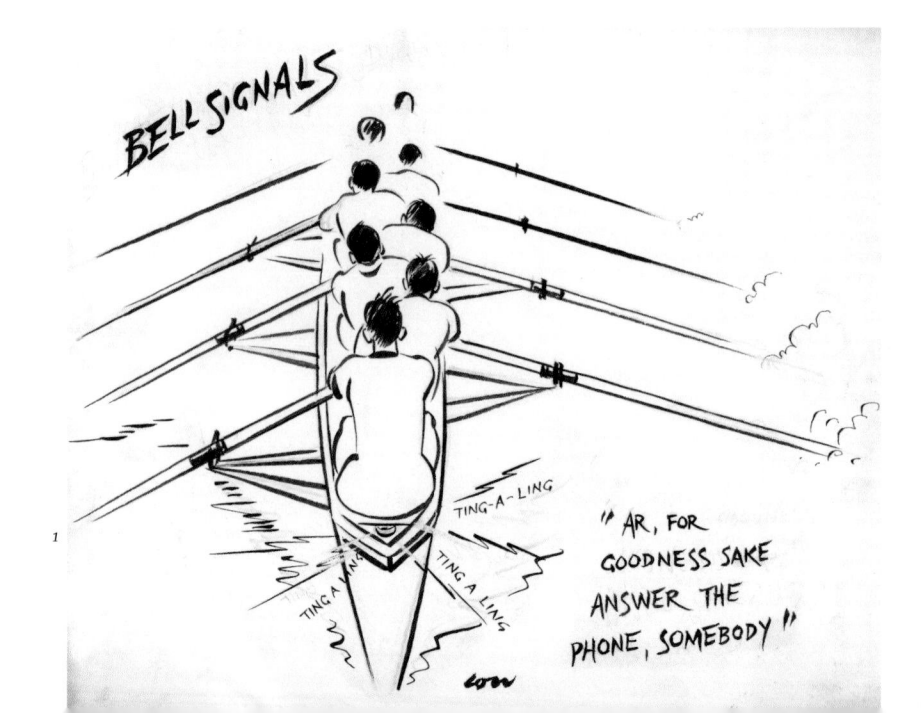

1 *David Low in the Evening Standard, 1933*

2 *Through Barnes Bridge, 1995*

Stage setting and management *continued*

The job of the London Representative has nothing to do with selection and training of the crews and everything to do with acting as 'impresario' to mount the race on the day and to find, negotiate with and look after the sponsor. It encompasses making arrangements with the Port of London Authority and the Metropolitan Police; with four local councils; working out the timetable and safety instruction; taking account of the tide; finding sufficient launches for both the boat race and Isis-Goldie race; agreeing precise timings with BBC Television and the coaches (never easy!); making sure that there are proper media arrangements; providing stakeboats and reliable men to man them (also not easy); liaising with the umpires; finding flag men to drop flags at key points of the race for timing purposes; ensuring the finishing judge is equipped with launch and flag; making sure that the sponsor has what he needs and is happy, and handling any of the minor or major crises which inevitably emerge each year.

More often than not the arrangements run smoothly, although each year there is a different problem to deal with. These are usually minor but from time to time a major crisis happens. In my first year, 1984, for instance, the Cambridge cox managed to steer his crew at full tilt into a fifteen foot high moored barge in the final practice just before getting on to the stakeboat, damaging his boat, and causing us to row the race 24 hours later on the Sunday afternoon. Though we briefly considered trying to get a replacement boat from the Amateur Rowing Association at Hammersmith, there was not really much choice because of the state of the tide, and it was pretty much a case of telling everybody to come back the next afternoon. This was the first time the race had been rowed on a Sunday and resulted in a television audience which, after wall-to-wall television and press coverage of the sinking on the Saturday evening and Sunday morning, was our biggest ever at 14.5 million viewers. There are some silver linings, particularly for the sponsor!

Having driven his old Vauxhall in to London and purposely abandoned it on Vauxhall bridge, he decided to channel some of his daredevil spirit into racing Alice, a splendid 1926 Alvis sports car that enabled him to reach Henley from Magdalen in under twenty minutes. Bertie Eugster had purchased a 4.5 litre Bentley, Mike Ashley an Aston Martin and John Garton a Straight Eight Packard. These friends would vie in achieving the fastest racing times between the bridges of both places in order to reach Henley for the rowing.

John Lewes
on Jock Lewes, Oxford

The BLUES disappear at GUINNESS TIME

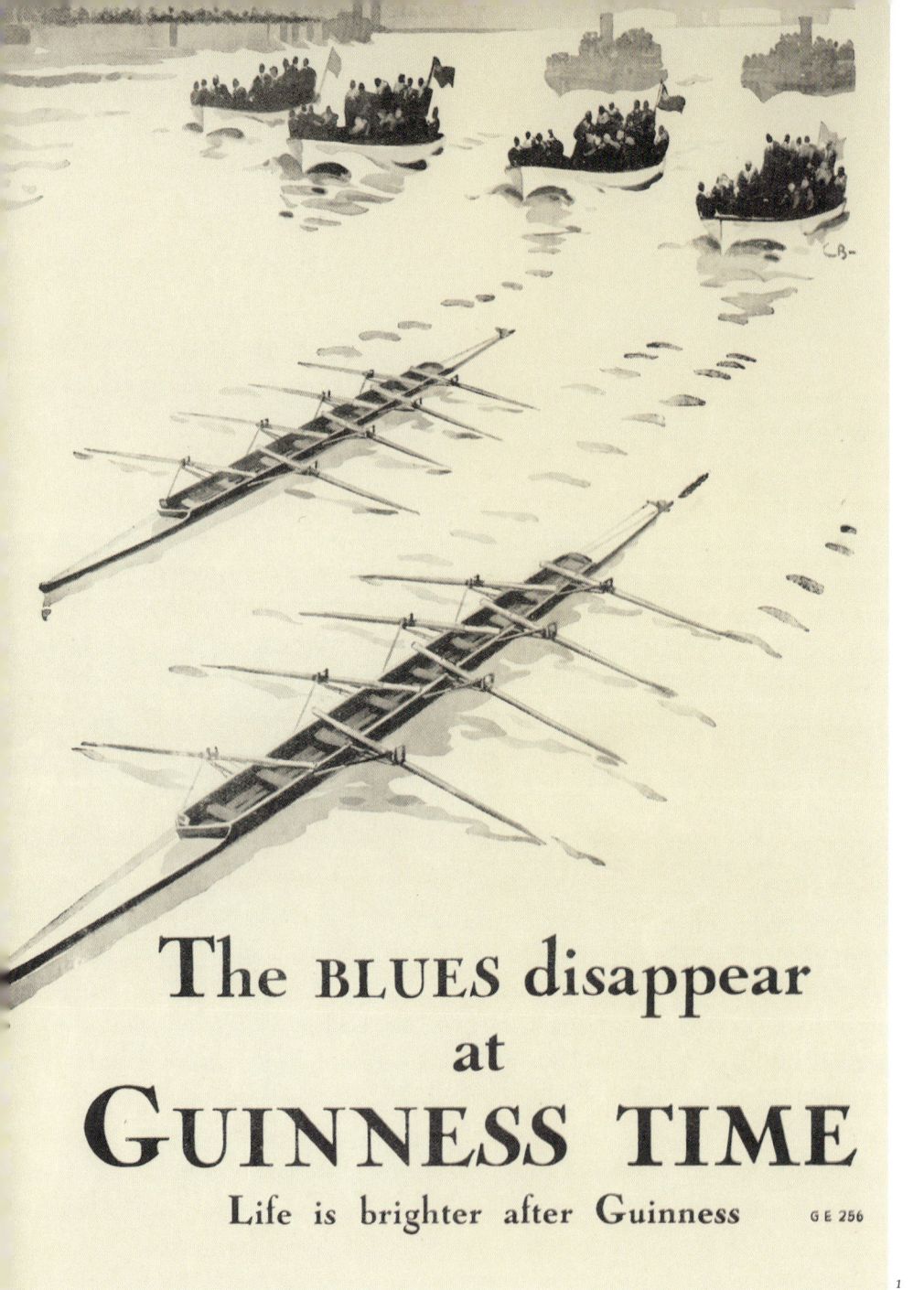

Life is brighter after Guinness

G E 256

Beware the orthodox, my son,
The slides that check, the arms that snatch;
Beware the drop-in blade, and shun
The Bourneish shoulder-catch.
Granta, 25 February 1927

1 Guinness poster

2 The Oxford mutineers, 1987, described by coach Mike Spracklen as 'the fastest Oxford crew I've ever seen'. Left to right: Tony Ward, Chris Clark, Tom Cadoux-Hudson, Gavin Stewart, Dan Lyons, Chris Penny, Richard Hull, Chris Huntington. Clark, Lyons, Penny, Huntington and cox Jonathan Fish opted out of the Boat Race

56 BATTLE OF THE BLUES

3 Chris Clark (centre) with Donald Macdonald behind him in 1986

4 Coach Mike Spracklen (left) with Oxford president Donald Macdonald, 1987

To be captain of a university eight requires qualities which would go some way to make a successful general… He ought to be a refined diplomatist, to have a rapid and decisive judgment, and the power of enforcing discipline. He should have the courage to hold firmly to his own opinion, and the rarer courage to make changes when it is necessary. A captain requires as much skill in composing a crew as a minister in forming his cabinet. It is not enough that the men separately should be good – and the breakdown of any one at a critical moment may ruin the whole plan - but each must fit into his proper place. There are infinite difficulties in soothing small vanities, and propitiating silly jealousies.

Leslie Stephen,
St Paul's Magazine, 1867

Mutiny tests loyalty   HUGH MATHESON

If you take any group of muscularly taut, monomaniac young men through whom the testosterone flows freely and fling them into a selection process which is physically hard and emotionally stressful, there are bound to be tears before bedtime.

The presidents' books throughout the 175 years of the Boat Race are full of tales of walkouts and resignations, of blows to the chin and all the emotional fallout of this tension. Usually it goes no further than the diary entry because the plaintiff decides that his ambition outweighs his grievance, and he gets back to work.

It is, however, peculiar that rowing an eight, where teamwork reaches its highest synthesis, also produces individuals for whom loyalty to the whole comes most definitely behind loyalty to number one.

Every now and again, however, we get a different social dynamic when a group of dissidents decides that their common interest is more important than the individual's in the scramble for places, and they try to force the establishment into a major change that suits their purpose.

For some reason, rowing revolutionaries seem to prefer dark blue. In the Michaelmas term of 1958 a huge squad began training at Oxford, including eleven blues from thirteen in residence plus some good younger men. Most of the British oarsmen had done National Service and were similar in age to the few postgraduates from abroad.

1920–1939

The 1927 race was closely fought until, passing Chiswick eyot, the Oxford number five, Hugh Edwards, cracked under pressure, and the light blues moved on to a five lengths win. Both crews had suffered from illness in the build up to the race, with Cambridge having to put Richard Craggs in as substitute only five days before the race. Oxford lost their stroke William Llewellyn with German measles a few days before the race, and then had the substitute Alan Hankin missing with a milder attack of the same illness until just before it. It is therefore remarkable that they managed to make such a good race of it, the light blues eventually winning by three lengths. This was the first race in which the BBC broadcast a running commentary.

In both 1928 and 1929 Oxford were in the doldrums and in the latter, centenary, year, Cambridge's sixth consecutive victory brought them level with Oxford again at 40 wins each. Oxford probably spoiled their chances of success in 1930 when, with a stronger squad than in the previous two years, an argument with his coaches gave rise to the resignation of president Alastair Graham. In 1931 neither crew was regarded as exceptional, but Cambridge put in a good performance on the day and won by two and a half lengths. 1931 was also the first year in which John Snagge was commentator (see Getting the News Out, page 69).

The year 1932 was interesting in two respects. In pre-war days Cambridge had turned to Oxford to seek coaching assistance on several occasions. This time the reverse took place, and John Gibbon from Cambridge coached 'rather second-class material' as the Oxford president, C M Johnston, described his crew. Gibbon coached Oxford on another three occasions, but never to victory. The 1932 race was won easily by a Cambridge crew which contained such stalwarts as David Haig-Thomas, Tom Askwith and Kenneth Payne. Harold Rickett and C J Sergel won the Grand at Henley in Leander colours, after which the Leander eight represented Great Britain in the Los Angeles Olympics, coming fourth.

At this stage Cambridge was still using fixed pin rowlocks on their riggers in the Fairbairn tradition. At a vote in 1933 they agreed to stick to this policy, and persisted with it in 1934. In 1934 they took the championship course record which had stood since 1911 down by 26 seconds to 18 mins 3 secs. Cambridge won by four and a quarter lengths, but Oxford, who were widely recognised as being the best dark blue crew for several years, were unlucky to come across such strong opponents, including Payne as president, Nick Bradley, Ran Laurie, Douglas Kingsford, Jack Wilson and the Australian Donald Wilson.

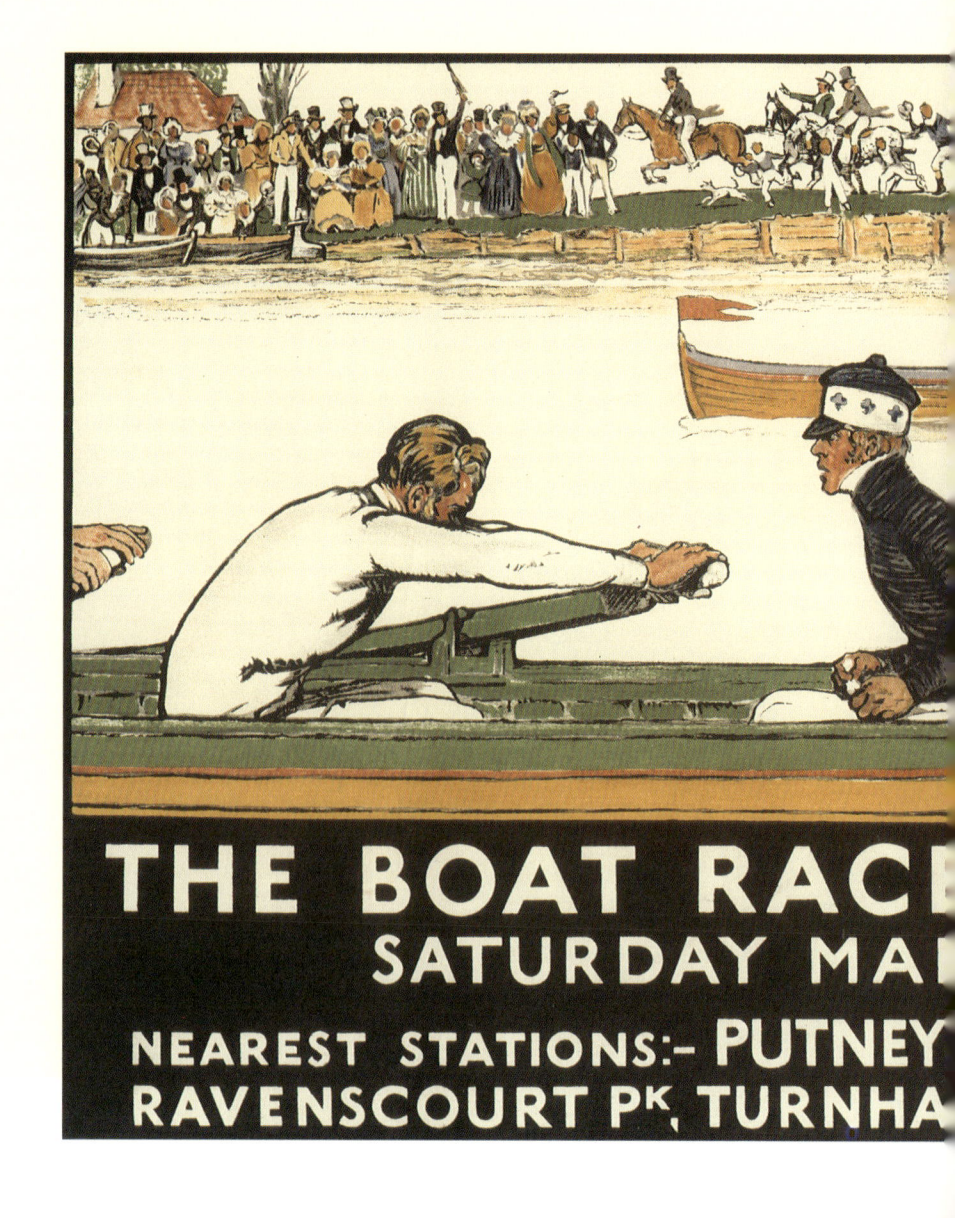

58 BATTLE OF THE BLUES

London Transport poster for the centenary race, 1929

Mutiny tests loyalty *continued*

The foreigners included Charlie Grimes, a 1956 Olympic gold medallist, and Reed Rubin who, like Grimes, was from Yale. The president, Ronnie Howard, had rowed for the 1958 Isis crew which, under the coaching of Jumbo Edwards, had frequently beaten the Blue Boat, which included Rubin, before it lost the Boat Race. His election as president over Rubin represented a vote for change.

Howard's first act was to invite Edwards to be his chief coach. Jumbo, while immensely gifted as an oarsman and inventive as a coach, also expected oarsmen to respond in a way that seemed childishly obedient to the older men. For example, Grimes bowed out because Edwards objected to the 'locomotive driver's hat' he wore for practice. With selection obviously so fraught, even for returning Blues, the squad split along the same fault lines that had divided the vote for president the previous May.

The dissidents called a press conference where they announced that they wanted to make a separate crew to be led by Rubin under a different coach and then to be given the right to race off with Howard's crew for the privilege of taking on Cambridge. Apparently the United States ambassador offered to back them with a boat, and the Yale coach was prepared to come over and guide the rebels.

Ronnie Howard, confronted by this direct challenge to his authority, went back to the people who had elected him the previous May and asked for a vote of confidence in his selected crew and in his decision not to race off. He won a resounding victory from the college captains, and the matter was closed. The Cambridge president also helped the establishment when he declared that his crew would race only the Howard eight. Three of the dissidents did return and helped Oxford record a six-length win.

1920 to 1939

The year 1935 saw a break by Bradley, the Cambridge president, from the old coaching methods, and fixed pins were dropped in favour of swivels. This led to three Cambridge coaches – Escombe, Payne and Peter Haig-Thomas – leaving to coach Oxford. In 1935 the race day was rough and Cambridge won the toss, which effectively sealed the result. In 1936 dark blue morale was rock bottom after a clash between the coaches and president R Hope, causing the latter to resign. As a result the disaffected Cambridge coaching team were denied a serious chance to prove their worth at Oxford. However, this was the thirteenth and last successive Cambridge victory, perhaps due to over-confidence, perhaps to their change in coaching.

1937 was an interesting one in boat race history. The Oxford squad was not a brilliant one, but they had a president, the Australian Jock Lewes, who, though not an outstanding oarsman, rebuilt morale and had the perception to see that the crew moved better without him. He therefore dropped himself. Cambridge, on the other hand, had potentially a very good squad but suffered the bad luck of losing Ran Laurie, the president and stroke, when he took up a post in the Sudan. Douglas Kingsford, another British Olympic oarsman, had to go down unexpectedly, and Hugh Mason, a good reserve stroke, broke his leg, although he returned just before the race to the number two seat. Perhaps more significantly, the crew which still had several highly competent oarsmen did not get together, probably because they were torn into two groups who favoured conflicting styles, orthodox and Fairbairn. The race was a close one, with changing fortunes until Chiswick, but Oxford then went ahead at the crossing and won by three lengths.

With their morale re-established, Oxford, who were coached for the first time by John 'Freddie' Page, who had done wonders for Oriel College over many years, also won the 1938 race, holding the lead through most of it and winning by two lengths. The first television broadcast of the event was attempted in 1938, rather unsuccessfully (see In Camera page 81).

As a result of their performances in the previous two years coupled with difficulties experienced by the Cambridge president Alan Burrough in sorting out his crew, Oxford went into the 1939 race as favourites. Surprisingly Cambridge, on the Surrey station, slipped away from them off the start, were a length up at the mile and steadily increased their lead to win by four lengths.

Cambridge moved from being six wins down on Oxford in 1914 to six ahead in 1939. During the 1939 to 1945 war, four unofficial races took place, two at Henley, one at Ely and one at Radley (see page 62).

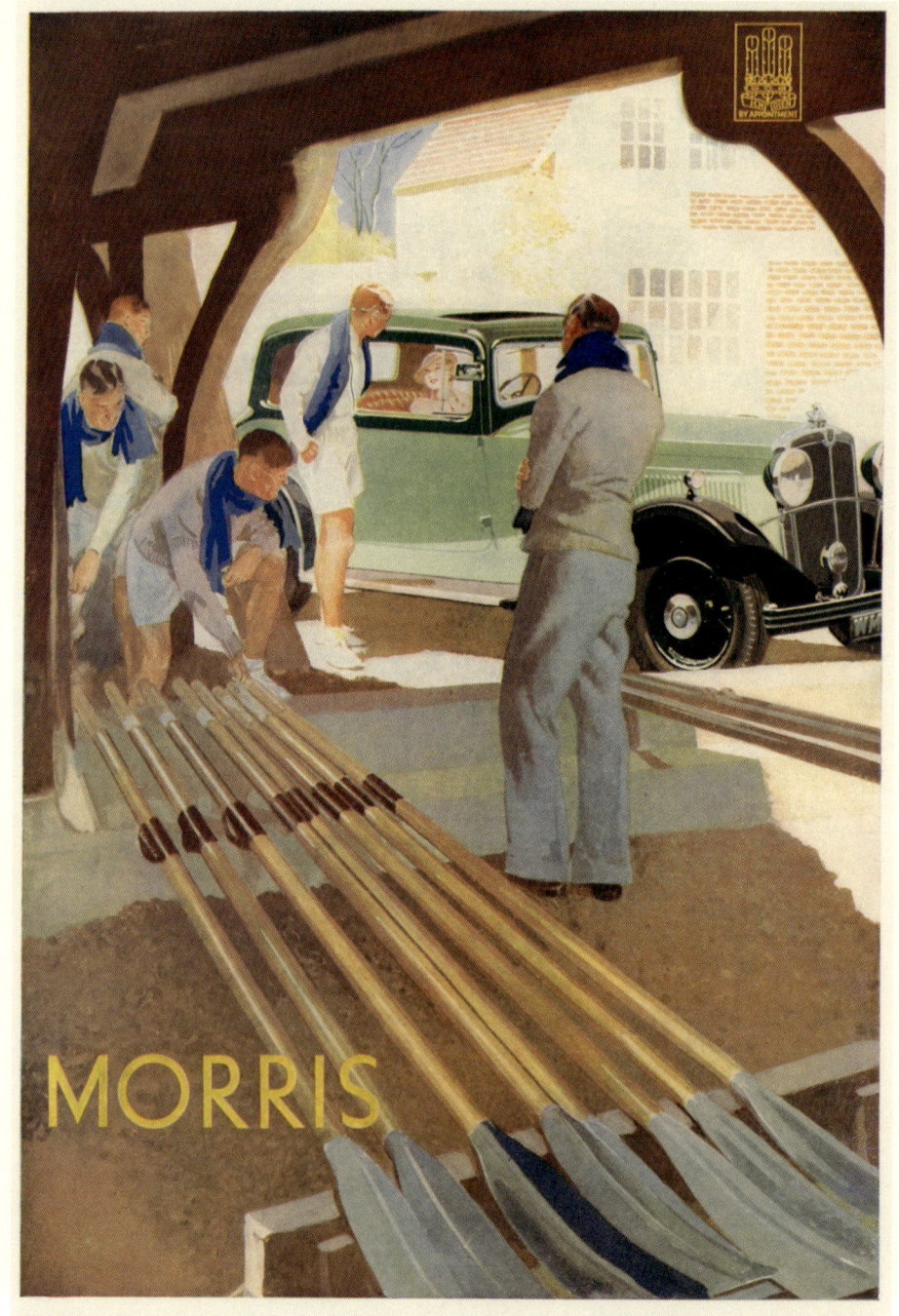

MORRIS

THE CAR WITH THE LOWEST UPKEEP COSTS

60 BATTLE OF THE BLUES

Jock left the Ranelagh Club for the West End sporting his silver coach horn; he gave a demonstration of the instrument from the roof of an OUBC vehicle in diverse locations, the most popular being Piccadilly Circus, where thousands of additional revellers were gathering. Extra police were drafted in to monitor the swelling crowds, and at one stage twenty stalwart policemen formed a close cordon round Eros.

John Lewes on Jock Lewes, Oxford

1 Advertisement from *Britannia & Eve*, 1935

2 Alan Burrough, Cambridge president in 1939. He dropped the Olympic champion Jack Beresford from his coaching team because in 1938 he had done little but provide beer

Mutiny tests loyalty *continued*

Almost thirty years later the old blues in residence proposed Donald Macdonald, a 31-year-old Scot as their leader, and the college captains duly elected him president of OUBC in May 1986. He did not fit the usual presidential mould. He won his blue in 1986 after a decade working in insurance while living and racing at London Rowing Club before deciding that he wanted the same degree in English that his wife had taken ten years before. He came up to Oxford aged 29. In 1986 he and a large blond Californian, Chris Clark, contributed to the first loss for Oxford and chief coach Daniel Topolski in eleven years.

Macdonald, who like every president before him had sole responsibility for choosing a chief coach who would set the style of his year in charge, stuck with the established winning team and reappointed Topolski. Crucial to the shape of the squad were four new Americans who, partly on Clark's encouragement, had arrived to avenge the dark blue defeat. These men were older and more confident of their own worth than the homegrown undergraduates.

Through the Michaelmas term they trained sometimes enthusiastically but sporadically and by their own admission not always to the Topolski regime, which they found irksome and felt was more suitable to schoolboys than the internationals they were – Chris Penny an Olympic medallist, Dan Lyons a world champion, and Chris Huntington and cox Jonathan Fish also having worn US shirts.

By the time of trial eights and in the Christmas break, which Topolski as always kept to a minimum, tension rose between the small group gathered round Macdonald, which took the letter of the training and testing law literally, and others who took the spirit of the regime seriously but baulked at returning early in the vacation and rowing at what they felt were unsocial hours.

WARTIME RACES

During the Second World War there were sufficient students of 'reserved status' in essential subjects available in each university to pick representative crews for a race in four of the six years between the 1939 and 1946 boat races. The normal three-year courses were sandwiched into two years, and training was restricted to three outings a week by agreement. Even these were undertaken with difficulty because of the lack of petrol to get to a useful stretch of water. Perhaps a greater restriction to serious training was food rationing. The abiding memory of the wartime oarsmen is the hunger that they experienced after training.

The 1940 race was at Henley over the 1908 Olympic course of 2000 metres, rowing against the stream in this late winter period. Oxford won the toss and chose the Bucks station. Cambridge went ahead soon after the start and gradually drew out to win by five lengths.

No races could be organised in either 1941 or 1942 but it proved possible to organise a race at Sandford over a narrow one and a quarter mile course from the black bridge to the island just above Radley College boathouse. Oxford again won the toss and chose the Oxfordshire side.

They set off at a fast pace and secured a lead of about one length after the first half-minute. Cambridge got into their stride and came back at them gradually, and the umpire's decision at the finish was a win for Oxford by two-thirds of a length.

In 1944 a race was organised over the Adelaide course of about one and a half miles on the River Ouse just outside Ely. As might be expected in February in the fens, it was a bitterly cold and miserable day. Cambridge went off well and by about halfway were ahead by about a canvas. However Oxford then came back and won by three-quarters of a length.

The final wartime race was at Henley again in 1945, this time on the Grand course rather than the Olympic one, and in better weather conditions than 1944. On this occasion Cambridge won the toss, chose Bucks, went off fast and established a lead which Oxford could not pull back. Cambridge won by two lengths. Thus the wartime races finished all square at two wins each.

The most interesting feature of contemporary accounts is the number of spectators assembled for each and every race, despite travel difficulties. Even in wartime the boat race did not lose its strange appeal.

62 BATTLE OF THE BLUES

1 Crews at practice, 1932

2 Programme for centenary Boat Race, 1929

Mutiny tests loyalty   *continued*

Contact between the two groups broke in early January. Each day after training Macdonald would return to his wife and children in north Oxford while the dissidents descended on the Oriel bar to contemplate their difficulties.

The crisis blew up over Topolski's decision to row Clark on bow side where the squad was weaker and to leave Macdonald on stroke side. This followed a famous 'seat race' in freezing weather at Henley. In seat racing the crews of two fours are instructed to row at constant ratings while the athletes being examined are swapped between them. The one who clocks up most advantage by winning in any combination attracts the selector's nod. It is certainly the best way of finding the boat movers within any group, even if its evidence is contrary to the other standard tests. It is also wide open to abuse. If an athlete who is not being tested prefers A to B he can act to put his choice in front. The argument over the Clark/Macdonald seat races will never emerge from the freezing spray and mist of that Henley afternoon in mid-January 1987.

Clark and his allies insisted that he had beaten Macdonald, that he should not row on bow side and that instead Macdonald should stand aside for him to row with his friends. Topolski was convinced this was a mistake and would produce a slower crew. He exercised his position as chief coach to select the crew he felt was best and resisted claims about the seat race by counter-charging that none of the rules about ratings or holding other things equal had been obeyed. When his view had been clearly expressed Clark and the group which had formed around him refused to row with the squad and, like the rebels thirty years before, suggested a takeover.

Styles in rowing are like seasons in Australia, bad, damned bad and bloody awful.

Steve Fairbairn, Cambridge 1882, 1883, 1886 and 1887 and coach in 1920. In 1882 and 1883 he was beaten by two of orthodoxy's greatest apostles, G C Bourne and R S de Havilland.

SWINGS OF FORTUNE

The period 1946 to 2003 can be split into two parts, pre- and post-1975. The first 30 races after the 1939 to 1945 world war consisted of a few short winning streaks by one or other university. Neither university established supremacy for more than the six years achieved by Cambridge from 1968 to 1973. After 1975 one or other achieved victories for long consecutive spells.

Rowing continued at both universities in wartime, though at a reduced intensity, so it was decided to resume the boat race on the tideway in 1946. Several of the available men had rowed in a wartime race. The time allowed for training remained restricted. Richard Turner Warwick was president at Oxford and John Paton Philip at Cambridge. Peter Haig-Thomas, Richard Eason and David Raikes coached for Oxford and Claude Taylor, Sidney Swann and Banner Johnstone for Cambridge. Of these Haig-Thomas, who coached Cambridge and subsequently Oxford before the war, was the only regular pre-war coach. This year was also notable for having the first third generation blue in Richard Bourne, who was son of R C and grandson of G C. Cambridge had a weight advantage of over seven pounds per man and came to the start as favourites. Oxford, on Middlesex, were ahead from soon after the start and as they approached Hammersmith moved over to take their rivals' water. Cambridge made strenuous efforts to displace them but to no avail, and Oxford went away to win by three lengths.

Cambridge then came back with a series of five wins. In 1947 they had a weight advantage of the same order as that in 1946. In sluggish river conditions due to the heavy flow of land water, the light blues won by ten lengths in 23 mins 1 sec, one of the slowest of all boat races.

Jumbo takes a spade to the water

Jumbo Edwards introduced us to spade blades early in training for the 1960 boat race. One evening he showed us a little contraption he had created, using two model oars, about nine inches long. One had the traditional blade shape, and one was what became known as a spade blade. This was a little squarer than the European barrel blade of the time.

Jumbo's contraption was a bowl of salt or sugar, I cannot remember which, representing the water. The model oar was held by a small, moveable frame representing the rigger and gate. The oar was placed in the salt at the beginning of the stroke, and Jumbo moved it through its arc as in rowing a stroke, whilst at the same time moving the rigger to represent the boat's forward momentum. At the end of the stroke a pile of salt remained behind the blade area, representing water built up as a result of the back-washing effect of the blade on the water.

The exercise was repeated using the spade blade. The resulting pile of salt was smaller because the shorter but fatter spade blade offered less back-wash resistance where the blade joined the loom or shaft of the oar. We were all immediately convinced of what was to us an unexpected benefit of spade blades.

Richard Bate, Oxford 1960

1 *Jumbo Edwards, Oxford coach, spade blade inventor*

2 *David Low in the Evening Standard, 1933*

Mutiny tests loyalty *continued*

When he was challenged Macdonald reacted in the same way as Howard by appealing to the college captains who had elected him, but not before the battle had captivated the public's taste for controversy in sport. On front pages and in prime time the two sides stoked up the frankly silly squabble about who had, or had not, been pulling harder in seat races, the process of which was not understood by the public.

In most of the media the dispute became, quite falsely, the 'rocket fuel' from the United States versus the verbally diffident but steely determined Macdonald and his tiny band of supporters. The college captains were much less reliably behind Macdonald and subjected to some excitable and almost promiscuous lobbying. A meeting of captains brought forth unexpected representatives of colleges which had not been evident on the Isis for many years, or in the case of the Jesuit foundation Campion Hall, ever. Campion formed a boat club and elected a novice priest, Michael Suaraez, as its captain because he persuaded the faculty of the injustice of the position he felt Macdonald had been put in. Ironically he was American. There were also frenzied approaches to the captains of all the women's clubs, which would certainly not have been part of Howard's calculations thirty years before.

The debate was memorably articulate and rolled around for two and a half hours before Macdonald eventually won the vote by 28 to 11. He started again trying to form a crew, although it was now desperately close to the race. Clark had already resigned from squad, and Macdonald lost the three other big Americans and his likely cox. A series of defeats on the tideway brought his motley crew to the start as clear losers.

Chris Barton was selected as Cambridge stroke in 1948. Training must have been an interesting experience, for he was a Fairbairn adherent who converted to an orthodox style for the boat race, reverted to Jesus style again for Cambridge's May bumping races and back to orthodoxy for the 1948 Olympics. Shortly after the start in a fresh north-north-east wind, Paul Bircher, the Cambridge six, caught a bad crab and the boat jolted to a halt. Oxford failed to take advantage and the light blues settled down again and took the lead at the mile. From there on the main interest lay in the question of the record, which Cambridge ultimately took by thirteen seconds in 17 mins 50 secs, to win by five lengths.

The 1949 race was very exciting and was the first to be televised in its entirety. Cambridge had a strong engine room with three Olympians, Brian Lloyd, Paul Massey and Bircher. Two excellent strokes were opposed, Chris Davidge for Oxford and David Jennens for Cambridge. They were good oarsmen, showed the character necessary to win a close race, but coupled with good sportsmanship. Harold Rickett had returned to coach Cambridge in 1948 and would take them through to 1952. Oxford surprisingly chose Middlesex. At the mile they were just over a length ahead but by Hammersmith had gained little more and had the outside of the long bend. Into a headwind along Chiswick reach, Cambridge edged up but by Chiswick steps, they had not taken adequate advantage and Oxford appeared likely winners. At the crossing Jennens pushed hard and began to overtake. At Barnes bridge, with Cambridge on the outside, the boats were level. Never had a crew on Surrey won unless they were in the lead at Barnes bridge. Both crews spurted all the way from Barnes but in the last ten strokes Jennens, supported particularly by Bircher and Massey, just managed to pull ahead to win by a quarter of a length.

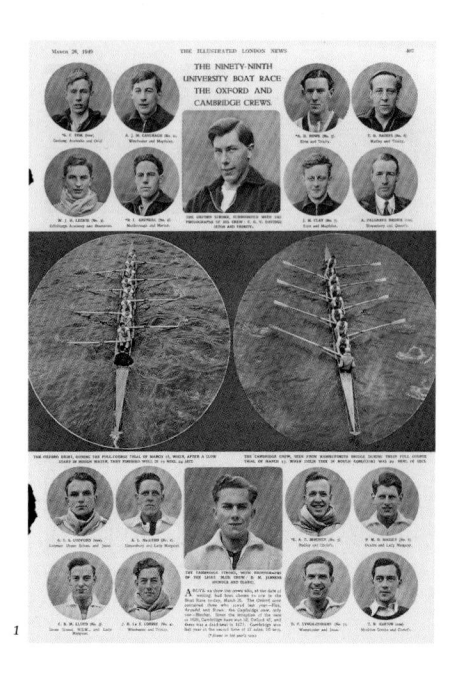

Coaching

There are only two styles. One is called winning, the other is losing.

*Donald Legget,
Cambridge coach 1996*

1. *Crew portraits in 1949, when David Jennens stroked Cambridge to win by a quarter of a length. Christopher Davidge stroked Oxford*

2. *Christopher Davidge comes ashore after stroking Oxford to win the 1952 race by a canvas. Coach Jumbo Edwards is also in the picture*

3. *Crews practise before the 1951 race in which Oxford sank at Putney. Jennens and Davidge were strokes as in 1949, and Cambridge won the re-row*

Mutiny tests loyalty *continued*

But he and Topolski had taken the boys away for a secret final week, and with a series of brilliant psychological games, which included as placebo a switch back to wooden oars and wrapping the hull in the same kind of cling film which had been used by the winner of a recent America's Cup, the coach transformed their attitude and capacity for victory.

Then, as the race was about to start, a thunderstorm of biblical proportions turned the tideway into the mid-Atlantic. Oxford, on Middlesex, shot straight from the start to the shelter of the Fulham wall and left Cambridge wallowing in the storm for a minute or two longer, just enough for them to ship too much water to be able to exercise their paper superiority and, although Cambridge were back in touch at Hammersmith, their blades had not been tempered in the same fire as had been burning for several months on the Isis. They slipped to a four-length defeat.

In Oxford the proposed reforms to make the boat race preparation more professional, which had been on hold throughout the mutiny year, were pushed ahead immediately. Chris Penny, a leading rebel, was elected president the following year and everything changed. Coincidentally, buckets more money came into the clubs from the BBC and sponsors, and presidents voluntarily relinquished many of their constitutional powers, including the appointment of chief coach, since when the risk of a blow-up of 1959 or 1987 proportions has all but disappeared.

BATTLE OF THE BLUES **67**

68 BATTLE OF THE BLUES

1 London Transport poster, 1955

2 John Snagge during his last commentary, 1980

3 John Snagge, BBC radio commentator, 1980

Getting the news out   CHRISTOPHER DODD

There is mayhem at the finish of the boat race. Reporters, cameramen and photographers mill about thrusting tape recorders, microphones and lenses in front of bedazzled winners and bedraggled losers, the latter's president trying to remain dignified among the ruin of his year's work. Losers soon vanish into the inner recess of their misery and their boathouse, and if you find one blubbing on the beach, half of you wishes that you hadn't.

Reporters who rode in the press launch huddle in the press centre to watch the television recording to confirm or clarify incidents, and the writing room fills with wordsmiths on laptops, mobiles and tight deadlines, and with photographers pumping pictures over the internet from their Apple Macs. There is a feverish adrenalin rush for an hour or two to conclude a day which began many hours before in the press centre at the start, where the sponsor provides brunch and the umpire gives a briefing before the ritual of the toss for stations and the anticipation of going afloat.

Like its spur to the development of amateur sport and the Corinthian spirit, the boat race's long association with the media remains hidden from the public except at the point of delivery. The television viewer, the radio listener or the newspaper reader may take for granted how their signal or printed page gets to them, but from its beginning the boat race has presented a challenge to all branches of the media, met with advances in technology and techniques of news gathering.

At least one reporter covered the first race in 1829 from the roof of a gatehouse beside Henley bridge. Others were probably on horseback to witness the clash and restart in the early stages of that race which would have been out of range of the man on the roof, even with a powerful telescope. When the race moved to the waters of Westminster and Wandsworth, a ride in a steamer was the only hope of seeing much of it. Clamouring steamers and river traffic was one of the causes of moving the race to its present Putney to Mortlake course in 1845, when press boats were already part of the entourage.

BATTLE OF THE BLUES   69

1946 to 1975

In 1950 Davidge, elected president, had the worst of the luck. Not only did jaundice force his withdrawal but Francis 'Two Legs' Hellyer who had coached Cambridge in their successful pre-war days, and Oxford in 1948 and 1949, died. Cambridge had six Lady Margaret men using fixed pins and their long lay back style. With Jennens, a Clare man put surprisingly at two and John Crick of Lady Margaret at stroke, they were too good for Oxford and won by three and a half lengths.

In 1951 Davidge, elected president for the second year, and Jennens were both back in the stroke seats, but this time Cambridge had the much more powerful crew. The Australian Brian Lloyd was president and Bill Wyndham, who rowed in 1947, was back at the university after National Service. The race was a fiasco. In a 'sinking wind' Oxford, who had won the toss and chosen Surrey, were waterlogged within a minute, with Cambridge paddling on in reasonable conditions in the shelter of the Fulham wall. The umpire Gerald Ellison, Bishop of Willesden, took the wise decision to declare 'no race', a decision which was subsequently endorsed in the rules, namely that there should be a re-row if any accidental event halted the race before the end of the Fulham wall. In the re-row on the following Monday, Cambridge moved rapidly ahead and won by twelve lengths. As a result of a prior invitation, the winning crew went to the United States and beat, separately, both Yale and Harvard crews and won the Revere Bowl.

In 1952, Jennens had gone down and James Crowden was elected president. Davidge was again the Oxford stroke. The race took place in a blizzard, with blinding snow, and a strong wind, luckily easterly so that the water conditions were not too bad. This time Cambridge chose Middlesex and both crews rowed along the Fulham wall. Cambridge were just ahead at the mile but level as they shot Hammersmith bridge. All round the Surrey bend Oxford tried to shake them off to no avail, nor could the light blues use the Duke's meadows bend to their benefit. The crews went through Barnes bridge side by side, a repeat of the 1949 race, but this time with Oxford on the outside of the bend. Once again the Surrey crew 'did the impossible' of winning by a canvas in the last few strokes after being level at Barnes, and Davidge got his revenge.

Oxford won the 125th race in 1979 and former prime minister Harold Macmillan had this to say: 'I hope – but of course as chancellor of the University of Oxford I have to be careful – you will go out and generally break up the town. If Piccadilly Circus stands tomorrow I shall be disappointed. If Eros has not been moved, or draped with suitable decorations, it will not be a good night.'

Harold Macmillan after Oxford won the 125th race, 1979

Diet and training in 1866, Cambridge regime

7:00 *Out of bed, piece of biscuit, run a mile at top speed (some walk).*

8:30 *Breakfast – hot or cold beef, mutton or chicken, boiled eggs, watercress, bread and butter; two cups of tea with milk and sugar (one nearer the race).*

9:30 *College work.*

1:00 *Lunch – meat, bread and butter, glass of sound beer. Some go for heavy meal.*

2:30 *Outing of 8 to 14 miles at slow rate in 'tub-eight' until 2 to 3 weeks before race when they use a single-strake outrigger, rowing at top speed daily.*

5:30 - 6:00 *Dinner – beef, mutton and fowls on alternate days (hare on Sundays), roasted, potatoes, greens, one pint of ale, generally Magdalene ale. Plain rice pudding. Bread or crusts and butter, watercress ad libitum.*

After dinner, light reading and rest, even in a semi-recumbent posture, but sleep is forbidden.

7:00 *Two glasses of port (three for ailing men) or claret, one orange, hard biscuits in any quantity.*

9:30 *Cup of tea and slice of bread and butter, or porridge.*

10:00 *Bed.*

Training in Theory & Practice, 1866

70 BATTLE OF THE BLUES

A day in the life of Cambridge 2004 president, Wayne Pommen

5:50 Out of bed. Small breakfast of juice and cereal. Cycle to Goldie Boathouse gym.

6:30 - 6:45 Stretching. Recording of resting heart rates and body mass.

6:45 - 7:00 Exercises to strengthen 'core' muscles.

7:00 - 8:30 Endurance training on rowing ergometer, 60-80 minutes continuous.

8:30 - 9:00 Shower, cycle to college or home for breakfast of juice, cereal, toast, eggs, beans, hash browns, sausage, and fruit.

9:00 - 1:00 Lectures or other academic work. If possible, a nap of 30-60 minutes is desirable during the morning.

1:00 Quick lunch, typically a baguette sandwich, juice or soft drink, and a cookie.

1:15 Cycle to Goldie Boathouse and minibus to Ely.

2:00 Stretch, review outing plan, identifying goals and points of emphasis.

2:30 - 4:30 On-water in singles, pairs, fours, or eights, depending on phase of training and time of year. Nearing the race, the majority is done in eights with set crews. A typical outing during the fall and winter is continuous endurance row of up to 22 kilometres at UT2 or UT1 intensity.

4:30 - 5:00 Discuss the outing. Stretch, shower, change.

5:00 Snack, carbohydrate and/or protein-rich food, water or energy drink.

5:30 Cycle home from Goldie Boathouse.

6:00 - 7:00 Dinner at college or home-cooked, content largely left to the oarsman. A standard meal would be pasta with meat sauce, vegetables, and bread, with a pudding to follow. Water, milk, or juice to drink. Alcohol avoided on most days.

7:00 - 10:00 Study, reading, internet surfing, video games, movies, or some other form of relaxation. Snack of cookies/fruit/pudding/cereal. Water is consumed frequently to maintain hydration.

10:00 Bedtime.

---

1 Cambridge crew, 1867

2 David Low in the Evening Standard, 1933

Getting the news out *continued*

This was a period when rowing was a popular spectator sport in London, a time before modern sporting attractions came on the scene, and a time of press expansion and enterprise hand in glove with a growing literate population. Rowing matches were popular and plentiful in London, from apprentices' races to the world professional sculling championships, and when gents from the landed aristocracy, the leading schools and the universities of Oxford and Cambridge came along to race in eight-oared boats, punters and populace alike grasped the opportunity of an argument and a flutter. Particularly the light and dark blues, who somehow captured the imagination of Londoners and then, through the newspapers and telegraph, the country as a whole.

In 1869 there was media frenzy when Harvard sent a four-oar to race Oxford over the boat race course. The transatlantic cable had just been laid to connect Volunteer Bay, Cork, with Heart's Content, Newfoundland, and copious despatches were filed to British and American papers for a month before the race by an illustrious band of reporters which included Thomas Hughes, author of Tom Brown's Schooldays, Charles Dickens, who presided over the feast which followed the race at Crystal Palace, and George Smalley, father of foreign correspondents. New York papers devoted most of their front pages to Harvard's defeat on the day, except for Smalley's, when the telegraph company failed to send his incredibly expensive despatch of 2,200 words. Estimates of the crowd reached one million. For the boat race itself, newspapers and agencies went to ingenious lengths to be first with the news on the streets.

The pundits got the 1953 race totally wrong. At Oxford morale was high after the previous win and during training things went well. Cambridge, coached by Crowden, Roy Meldrum and Jennens until finished by Ronnie Symonds at Putney, were much criticised, though it was recognised that the Harvard man Louis McCagg had considerable power. The crews came to the start with Oxford as favourites. Cambridge led from almost the first stroke, gradually moved further ahead and won by eight lengths.

The 1954 race was the hundredth in the series and both crews experienced difficulties during the preparations with frozen rivers; but a greater problem was that several old blues were sent down for a poor academic record. The race was a level one to Hammersmith but in Chiswick reach Oxford were on the sheltered shore while their rivals butted into and coped poorly with a head wind, allowing Oxford through to win by four and a half lengths.

Cambridge then had a run of four wins in succession. The first of these was a sad race for Oxford, who were giving away over 10lb per man. Up to Hammersmith they were very much in contention, but in Chiswick reach, two Oxford men, E O G Pain and J G McLeod, were in trouble to the extent that McLeod blacked out. Cambridge immediately spurted away and won by 16 lengths.

No nation in the world (except our brother Anglo-Saxons across the Atlantic) has such a crown to its pleasures as our university boat race, which has – among the upper classes, at all events – supplanted even the Derby.

Illustrated London News, 20 March 1875

72 BATTLE OF THE BLUES

1 Cambridge practise on the Housatonic River, Connecticut, before beating Yale, 1951

2 Pluck magazine

Getting the news out *continued*

Correspondents on the press steamer would seal reports in airtight tin boxes and throw them to a boy in a dinghy who would paddle off to the telegraph office. In 1898 the Post Office placed horse-drawn post offices near the Duke's Head in Putney and near the winning post. Pencils and telegram forms were provided, and operators in the van manned Wheatstone instruments wired to the mains which tapped out messages in Morse on rolls of green paper. The Post Office recorded more than 120 messages sent from the Duke's Head office and 250 more from the permanent Putney office.

Before the era of photography, illustrated papers such as the Graphic and the Illustrated London News honed pictorial depiction of the race to a fine art. A vista at Hammersmith or Barnes would be prepared in advance, sometimes joined up in sections executed by more than one artist, and the position of the boats would be added at the last minute. In 1890 Scientific American ran a feature on how pictures were sent by carrier pigeon to the offices of the Daily Graphic.

Pigeons were also used from the bank during the race or at the finish to fly the verdict direct to newspaper offices or telegraph offices at Barnes and Richmond. And the birds also connived at betting scams by being released before the end of the race to fly to accomplices with the appropriate colour ribbon of the leader tied to a leg. In 1865 a pigeon launched from Hammersmith where Cambridge were leading reached Hampton Court wearing a light blue tag, but Oxford took the race by four lengths and kept the bookie happy.

The Exchange Telegraph company laid their own field wire along the course and had cyclists stationed at key points. Signalmen borrowed from the Guards were stationed at strategic bankside points to compile a 'runner'. 'Heigh presto', said the Westminster Gazette, 'the result was in New York in half a minute.'

Oxford with McLeod president were also giving away weight in 1956 but now the difference was just over seven pounds per man. This year Cambridge were already up by one and a half lengths at Hammersmith, but Oxford on Middlesex held them to this gap until the crossing. They did not have enough power to force Cambridge out as they came along Duke's meadows and despite some good drives by Oxford all the way to the finish, the light blues held on to win by one and three-quarter lengths.

1957 was a very interesting year. An Australian, Roderick Carnegie, was president at Oxford and changed to what was then known as American rig with radically heavy gearing by the standards of the day. He also pushed stamina training in a crew which was the heavier by seven pounds per man. Oxford came to the start as favourites. On Middlesex, they were a length up at the mile but Cambridge had pulled back by Hammersmith and were a few feet ahead. As the crews moved along Chiswick reach, the Oxford five man Peter Barnard was clearly under-performing and the light blues moved out to a three-second lead at Chiswick steps. Cambridge gradually moved further ahead to win by two lengths. In 1958, Cambridge were the stronger crew and on a foggy, rainy day they rowed away steadily to win by three and a half lengths.

The start of the year 1959 saw a short-lived revolution at Oxford in which the resident blues tried to dispose of the president Ronnie Howard and his chief coach Jumbo Edwards and replace him with a coach from Yale. However, the captains' meeting supported the president, Cambridge announced that they would only race against the president's crew, and the revolution collapsed. Oxford turned out a crew which was far too strong for the light blues, going away from them at the start and winning by six lengths.

Oxford again had the better crew in 1960 and for the first time used spade blades. They went off well on Middlesex and were ahead by three seconds at the mile. From there on despite everything Cambridge tried, the dark blues held on tenaciously to win by one and a quarter lengths. Following this performance the Oxford eight, with the exception of their president David Rutherford, who strained his back, rowed as Great Britain in the 1960 Rome Olympics.

The 1961 race looked as though it would be a quiet row-over for Oxford, which had five members of the 1960 Olympic crew available, while at Cambridge president John Beveridge was one of only two remaining blues. But Beveridge had two Harvard men, Mark Hoffman at stroke and Michael Christian at seven. Oxford set off well on Surrey and were up by a length at Hammersmith and one and a quarter at Chiswick steps. Then at the crossing the Oxford number six, Graham Cooper, dropped his head and almost stopped rowing. Hoffman took the initiative and slipped through and although Cooper picked up the stroke again, Cambridge moved on to an unpredicted victory by four and a quarter lengths.

Clothing should consist of merino jerseys of a moderately thin texture; one or two thick knitted woollen jerseys to wear over thinner ones when practising in cold weather; a flannel or pilot-cloth boating-coat warmly lined, in which it is well to have a band of elastic round the wrists to prevent the wind blowing up the arms in cold, windy weather; flannel caps, woollen comforters, straw hats, flannel trousers, and thin white shoes worn over ordinary woollen socks.

The Arts of Rowing and Training, 1866

Advertisement from the Illustrated London News, 1933

Getting the news out *continued*

One of the great wheezes was the use of rockets, whereby a man would fire a rocket of a pre-ordained colour to signal to his colleague at the telegraph office which crew was in the lead. This scheme was sundered when a rival publication got wind of it and sent a 'pyrotechnic enthusiast' to sow confusion by launching several dozen rockets at the same time. 'The face of the rival, who had to receive the signals at Mortlake, when he saw the display, was tragic,' said J B Booth in A Pink'Un Remembers.

In 1906 the Cambridge Daily News crowed that it had the edition containing the result on sale at 12.26 pm, – four minutes after the winner crossed the line. 'A few minutes later a second special edition was issued containing a full report of the race.'

Such split timing and ingenuity mattered when newspapers were the only means of getting the news out, when an editor's aim was to be first with the news and scoop his rivals. Between the wars, Bill Evans of the Star, who was also a pilot, tried to persuade his office to allow him to report the race from an Autogyro, a kind of forerunner of the helicopter. 'I worked out exact details, including having my report phoned from a call box at the airport at Heston, where Autogyros used to be headquartered, and having my car there to take me to Twickenham, where so often on the same afternoon the England v Scotland rugby international was played,' he wrote. Unfortunately his editors were not impressed.

The coming of radio, and later television, began to change all that. Radio could almost always be first with the news, and so for the newspapers the battle lines shifted to detail, analysis, investigation, comment and personality. These remain the main ingredients of competition in the twenty-first century.

The year 1962 saw Jumbo Edwards change the Oxford plan to include a substantial amount of interval training (alternate low and high power) after the collapse of crew members in previous years, while Cambridge concentrated on technique, particularly because they had to incorporate two overseas oarsmen, Boyce Budd from Yale and John Lecky, a Canadian Olympian. The crews were level at Hammersmith but as they moved into a headwind and rougher water in Chiswick reach, Oxford suffered more from the conditions on the outside of the bend and were behind by more than two lengths at Chiswick steps. Cambridge eventually won by five lengths.

Winter 1963 was a wretched one, with severe frosts making training difficult for both crews. On race day there was virtually no stream due to the land water flow and Crabtree reach sported a strong headwind. Oxford, the heavier crew by over seven pounds per man, moved through it better and were ahead on Surrey by two seconds at Hammersmith. With things in their favour the dark blues went on to win by five lengths.

The Cambridge crew in 1964 were firm favourites from an early stage. They had the Canadian Lecky, the American John Kiely and a very competent stroke in president Chris Davey. Nor did they disappoint, for they moved ahead from almost the first stroke and won by six and a half lengths.

1965 was effectively 1964 in reverse. The Oxford stern four were all from Yale – Fink, Howell, Spencer and Trippe – and Duncan Clegg, who became London Representative for the boat race from 1984 to 2004, rowed at three. Cambridge held them until the mile, but then the dark blues moved away and won by four lengths. The race in 1966, with Clegg as president for Oxford and Mike Sweeney who went on to become chairman of Henley Royal Regatta as president in Cambridge, was remarkably similar to the previous year even if the path to get there was different. Preparations were relatively problem-free in 1965, but 1966 saw much illness, the use by both crews of what was then known as the 'German rig', with four and five both rowing on bow side, and late selection. The race, too, was much closer as far as the crossing, but better Oxford watermanship enabled them to take the inside of the final bend to win by three and three-quarter lengths.

1 *Lou Barry, Cambridge coach 1968 to 1973*

2 *Cambridge beat milk rationing with a cow of their own, 1949*

I felt the shadow of Barnes bridge above us; in a few moments I should be able to smell the smell of the brewery. Surely, the smell of malt and of tar and of the tang of seaweed on the marshes are the three best smells in the world.

David Haig-Thomas
in I Leap Before I Look, 1936

Getting the news out *continued*

The first attempt at air-borne reporting came in 1939 when BBC radio hired an aeroplane. John Snagge, the commentator, who became the 'voice of the Boat Race' on the radio for fifty years, remembered that 'when we called it from the launch... the commentator, Seymour de Lotbiniere, was so violently airsick that all he said was "Cambridge are a good three lengths ahead. And now back to the launch".' Thrice more the BBC tried. On the second occasion Stewart MacPherson couldn't take off because of fog, on the third he couldn't see because of fog on the river, and on the fourth his aircraft caught fire, fortunately landing safely but without contributing to the commentary.

Radio commentary began in 1927 with Gully Nickalls and Sir John Squire as commentators, with four engineers, an assistant, a launch driver and a ship's engineer with 1000lb of transmitting equipment on board the Magician. The message was transmitted via an aerial slung between masts to four reception points along the river. Snagge began commentating in 1931. He was a former college oarsman and a career broadcaster, blessed with a voice of deep velvet and a nervous tension which never let him dry up in a life of live reporting of great state occasions. In a memoir published in 1953 he itemised some of the many disasters that befell the boat race commentator.

In 1949 his launch fell behind before Hammersmith bridge and did not catch up for two miles. His struggle to see the finish resulted in his best known, and only, gaff 'I don't know who's ahead, it's either Oxford or Cambridge'. The year before, in driving rain, visibility was atrocious and several gallons of water poured down Snagge's neck when his launch passed right under a land drain outpouring on Hammersmith bridge. The race was in the late afternoon, which meant that there was no time to get back to the studio for his Sports Report round up, so still in the pouring rain he returned aboard the open launch to Putney and there, lying out in the river, broadcast his account. In 1952, in a blinding snowstorm and about a mile from the finish, 'our launch broke down. And while we drifted helplessly on a popply Thames, Oxford were winning the race of the century unknown to us. It was galling to have missed a great finish and to be unable to broadcast a commentary as it happened or to talk about it later, but nothing could be done about it.'

1946 to 1975

At this stage Oxford had not won three races in succession since 1913, but this possibility existed in 1967. It was the year in which Dan Topolski, a future coach of distinction, won his first blue, rowing at 11 stone 11lb in the seven seat. The race was a close one until Hammersmith, with the dark blues always in front, but by not more than a length. In Chiswick reach, Cambridge, on Middlesex, tried to get past in rough water while Oxford sheltered under the bank. The light blues lost over a length by the crossing which enabled Oxford to take the inside of the final bend and win by three and a quarter lengths.

Cambridge's fight back began under president Patrick Delafield in 1968, resulting in six successive wins, the longest run that either crew had achieved since 1936. Both crews had a lot of experience, but the light blues were some six pounds a man heavier with a powerful engine room. The race was close to Hammersmith, but then Cambridge, on Surrey, made a determined push and by Chiswick steps were seven seconds ahead and won by three and a half lengths.

In 1969 Cambridge came to Putney as firm favourites with four blues from the previous year and David Cruttenden as the heaviest man to row in the race at 15 stone 11lb. They moved steadily ahead from the start and won by four lengths.

Despite the fact that Oxford, with cox Ashton Calvert as president, had five blues available against only one at Cambridge in 1970, the light blues came to the start as favourites. The race was notable for determined coxing by Calvert, who harassed his rivals all the way to the eyot, but without avail, Cambridge winning by three and a half lengths.

The 1971 race was described in the media as a great non-event. Cambridge with Christopher Rodrigues as president was exceptionally strong when compared to Oxford, who were in the doldrums. The light blues won by ten lengths in 17 mins 58 secs, the second fastest time on record. The situation was not much better for Oxford in 1972 when Cambridge moved ahead from their rivals at the mile and won by nine and a half lengths. In 1973 Oxford made their situation even worse by choosing Surrey in very rough conditions at Putney. With the dark blue boat carrying a substantial amount of water, Cambridge, who used the protection of the Fulham wall, rowed on to win by thirteen lengths.

In 1974 it was Oxford that had the distinctly stronger crew with the American Olympic oarsman David Sawyier as president, while Cambridge were missing some of their winning blues due to academic pressures. Cambridge chose Middlesex and with the help of the bend, managed to hold their rivals to less than a length to the Crabtree, but here Oxford took charge to win by five and a half lengths. The dark blue rejoicing was short-lived. Cambridge, with the blues who had stood down for academic reasons now back, reversed the race pattern of 1974 and won from Middlesex by three and three-quarter lengths. But this was the last race they were going to win until 1986.

Over the period 1946 to 1975, Oxford won ten races to Cambridge's twenty, making the overall score Oxford 52, Cambridge 68, with one dead-heat.

The Light Blue Lauries

William George Ranald Mundell Laurie, known as 'Ran', won the Olympic gold medal for coxless pairs with his partner Jack Wilson at the 1948 games in London, where the rowing took place at Henley-on-Thames. Laurie and Wilson formed their partnership at Cambridge where they rowed in three winning boat race crews from 1934 to 1936, breaking the record in 1934. In that year Laurie also stroked Leander Club to a record in the Grand Challenge Cup at Henley and stroked the British eight to fourth place in the Olympic Games in Berlin. His fourth child, Hugh, was born in 1959, and rowed for Cambridge in 1980 before becoming better known as an actor and comedian. He was about 12 when he learned of his father's Olympic success:

He pulled his gold medal (tin with gold leaf, as it happens – the war had rarefied everything) out of a sock at the bottom of a cardboard box. No frames, no glass cases – in fact hardly any rowing memorabilia on show in the house. Astounding humility, of a sort that people would barely comprehend nowadays.

Years later, I remember him as a half-way mark umpire, sitting under a square yard of canvas in blistering heat at Wallingford Regatta the entire day, Thermos and cheese sandwich at his feet, while glossier men gave prizes in the enclosure and rode in the launch. He had got a lot from rowing, and this was the giving back. And yet saying that makes him sound pious, as if sitting there all day was a self-consciously virtuous act, which isn't right at all. There was no sense of virtue about him. But by golly he was virtuous.

I remember rowing a pair with my father. I was a teenager in full-time training, six foot three and fourteen stone, he was a GP in his mid-fifties who did a spot of gardening, and I had to go like hell to keep the boat straight. The power, and the will, was almost frightening. He simply never paddled light. He would jump off that stretcher as if he meant to break it.

We also used to compete, in the most uncompetitive way, at a rather weird strength exercise: lying supine and lifting one's legs, straight, four inches off the floor and holding it – two minutes, three minutes, four minutes. I never beat him at it, even when he was well into his sixties. His physical strength was extraordinary. He was once assaulted in his surgery by a large man who punched him as hard as he could in the stomach. According to the receptionist who witnessed it, my father raised an eyebrow and told him to calm down.

Alf Twinn, the Cambridge boatman through most of the twentieth century, coached both me and my father. Not surprisingly, I didn't measure up in Alf's eyes. 'The thing about your Dad was, you never said anything to him twice. A lot of these gentlemen, supposed to have a brain, you say the same thing every day for three years and they never hear you. But your Dad – once only. He was the real thing.'

I have a picture over my desk of my father and Jack Wilson receiving their gold medals on the pontoon at Henley in 1948. Jack is loose-limbed and dashing, my father ramrod straight to attention. I think it describes the two of them very well – or perhaps each is describing a part of the other – for these were two really remarkable men. Tough, modest, generous and, I like to think, without the slightest thought of personal gain throughout their entire lives. A vanished breed, I honestly believe.

Hugh Laurie

1   Cambridge with Jack Wilson at seven and Ran Laurie at stroke, 1936

2   Hugh Laurie (centre), Cambridge 1980

Getting the news out continued

Brian Johnston, 'Johnners' to millions of cricket fans, joined the radio team in 1947 on a small wooden platform at Hammersmith bridge. After Snagge's disaster in 1952, Johnners spent the next 25 boat races at Chiswick bridge, taking over the commentary when the crews were sighted under Barnes bridge before handing back to Snagge for the finish. In 1977 he was on the launch for first time as linkman with the commentary points along the way, and in 1978 it was his launch which rescued the Cambridge oarsmen when their boat sank at Barnes. In 1980 he took over the commentary from Snagge and retired in 1989, along with Tom Sutcliffe, who supplied technical details while he described the action, after 42 years involvement with the race. Johnston recalled trouble over the team's rehearsals on the day before the race when, after lunch at the Star and Garter, they tested the equipment over the course with mock commentary, calling the crews Oxbridge and Camford and saying 'daft things'. Short wave radio listeners complained.

The next commentator, Peter Jones, collapsed on the launch during the 1990 race and died in hospital. David Mercer, the tennis commentator and a former rower, followed him, and Nick Mullins is the present incumbent.

The boat race has tested all branches of the media over its long history and remains as much of a challenge for the laptop artists of the printed word, the camera shutter, the ear of the radio and the eye of television as it was for men with notebooks and pencils in 1829.

BATTLE OF THE BLUES

In camera BARBARA SLATER

The boat race is a television director's dream. Any producer would relish the challenge of capturing the excitement, drama and tradition of this historic event. It is a privilege to sit faced with an array of monitors, all showing a different picture and angle and to try to keep up with the rapidly unfolding story. The race might take twenty minutes, but with the frenzy of talkback, radio communications, commentary and taking timings it feels as though it's over in seconds. Despite all the practice runs there is no real rehearsal, there are no second chances, there is only one race.

The boat race is one of the BBC's most complicated outside broadcasts, with radio signals positively bristling the air and beaming between boats via helicopter and satellite. It is a complex operation to mount and the four and a quarter mile course stretching out along the Thames presents a unique and formidable challenge; you can hardly run cables under the river!

It is planned like a military operation. Preparations for the next year start on the Monday after the race. Coverage incorporates mini cameras on the racing boats, a catamaran running alongside the crews and a radio camera with the umpire. A helicopter with a camera is flying above, and there are twenty cameras, some on hoists and cranes, spread between the tow path at Putney and the finish at Chiswick Bridge to ensure that the viewer at home misses nothing. A fleet of motorbikes whiz cameras from start to finish to obtain maximum use out of every facility. There is now a computer-generated virtual finish line and GPS satellite technology to track the boats.

1 Cambridge embark, 1999. Stroke – Tim Wooge, cox Vian Sharif

2 Putney reach at the start of the Boat Race

1946 to 1975

ISIS AND GOLDIE JOIN THE PARTY

The annual race between Isis and Goldie is now very much part of boat race day, but it was not always thus. The race between the reserve crews, having started in 1965, is a young interloper in the context of the boat race's 175-year history.

The Oxford reserve crew is named after the river flowing through Oxford, while Cambridge honour one of their great oarsmen John Goldie (a blue from 1869 to 1872) whose name is also associated with the university boathouse on the Cam. Isis and Goldie first appeared as names of crews during the inter-war years, though not to designate reserve crews.

The history of Isis is clearer than that of Goldie, though both were developed with the same broad purpose. For very many years there was a tradition that a crew could only be called Oxford or Cambridge if it was composed entirely of blues i.e. those who had rowed against the other place in an official race. There were, however, many occasions when a crew was entered for a regatta or sent on an overseas invitation visit. The Isis Club was established as a separate corporate entity for this specific purpose in 1927. Goldie was not such a formal arrangement, but came into being about the same time. On most occasions blues formed part of the crew, but there were periods when college oarsmen banded together to row under those names.

Until 1937 the remaining trialists returned to their college crews as soon as the university crew had been selected, and replacements were drawn back as necessary. Oxford were going through a bad patch in the 1930s, and in 1937 the non-rowing president Jock Lewes decided to keep the unsuccessful trial eight together at Putney until boat race day as competition for the blue boat.

In 1938 and for many years after the 1939-1945 war, crews of young hopeful college oarsmen trained with the university crew at Putney before the race, and they often rowed in head races and regattas. In the early 1960s it was proposed that these 'stalking horse' crews should race against each other as a prologue to the race. For a few years the idea was resisted on the highly suspect excuse that they would 'leave the water rough for The Race'!

However, in 1965 it was agreed to run a race between Isis and Goldie over the championship course thirty minutes before the boat race. The crews are now of undoubted talent, many oarsmen and coxes progressing to the blue boat in subsequent years, and a substantial number have achieved international status at under-23 level before they have been awarded a blue.

Of the 39 races to 2003, Isis have won 14 and Goldie 25. Goldie has also secured two sets of eight successive wins (1967-1974 and 1990-1997) against one run of four (1980-1983) by Isis.

Diet and training in 1866, Oxford regime

7:30 Out of bed, short walk.

9:00 Breakfast – chops, steak, egg, bread and butter, two cups of tea.

10:00 Reading and other duties.

1:00 Lunch – bread and butter, slice of cold meat near the end of training, occasional watercress and glass of beer.

Rowing – long course to Abingdon three times a week (8 miles), walk back to Nuneham (2 miles) and have the boat rowed for them, pull up to Sandford (3 to 4 miles from Oxford) return home on foot, running less than one mile.

Other days, twice to Iffley lock and back.

6:30 Dinner – roast beef and mutton, chops or steaks, fowl and fish, potatoes and greens, or light pudding occasionally, two glasses of beer, bread and butter and cress. two glasses of port with hard biscuits and one orange.

9:00 Cup of tea, chocolate or gruel.

10:30 Bed.

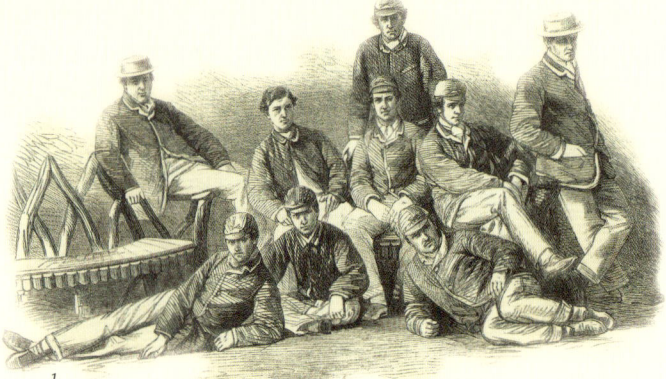

82 BATTLE OF THE BLUES

A day in the life of Oxford 2004 president, Sam McLennan

6:15 Out of bed, light breakfast, typically a bowl of cereal. 250g carbohydrate.

7:00 60-80 minutes ergometer/weight session in gym

8:30 Snack, typically bagel and two bananas

9:00 - 1:30 Free time for classes

12:00 Lunch 250-500 grams pasta with vegetables and sauce

1:30 Meet to drive to Wallingford, approx. 30mins.

2:30 On water for outing, 16-20 km row.

4:00 Off water, snack of honey sandwiches, 150g carbohydrate.

5:00 - 7:00 Study time in Oxford.

7:00 Dinner, high carb, pasta, rice, fish and vegetables.

8:00 Study.

10:00 Bed.

We aim to eat 5000 calories a day, 60 per cent carbohydrate. We don't drink alcohol daily or at all for about two months before the race. We train six days a week.

Recipe for beef tea

One lb of rump steak cut very fine and soaked for two hours in a pint of cold water, then put on the fire and allowed to come to the boil. Add a little salt, and strain.

1870s

1 Oxford crew, 1867

2 Radio Times 1933. BBC television coverage began in 1938 and terminated after the 2004 race

In camera *continued*

It is an intriguing contrast: the most modern high-tech digital technology being used to cover this most traditional event. But the coverage of the boat race has always been pioneering, even in the earliest days. The BBC's long association with the event started in 1927 with the first radio broadcast: a running commentary from Guy Nickalls and Sir John Squire. The legendary John Snagge made his first commentary in 1931 with Holt Marvel sandwiched between Children's Hour and International Rugby.

The first television coverage in 1938 was not achieved without a struggle. After a series of exchanges, Brentford and Chiswick Council agreed to reduce their charges for allowing the BBC to locate a mobile television unit on land near the river. For five guineas the BBC was able to secure positions for three cameras. Then a road builder accidentally drilled through cables in Muswell Hill, cutting off communications with the studio at Alexandra Palace and jeopardising the transmission, but eventually viewers were able to enjoy the drama with live commentary from the radio team complementing a chart and model boats!

A decade later the Radio Times proudly boasted 'for the first time in the history of television, viewers will be able to watch the entire length of the course' and 18 March 1949 saw the BBC launch one of its most ambitious broadcasts ever. After intensive testing a few days before the race, it was decided that a radio camera and transmitter would be installed on the launch Consuta to follow the crews, with a further eight cameras positioned along the river. Pictures from these mobile units were fed to a specially arranged control room at Broadcasting House. In comparison, a mere six cameras had covered the 1948 Olympics. In 1955 there were further advances and a helicopter, borrowed from British European Airways, was used for the first time.

BATTLES OF THE GIANTS

There are two features of note during the thirty years to 2003. First, for the last 27 of them the boat race has benefited from successive, understanding commercial sponsors – Ladbrokes, Beefeater Gin and Aberdeen Asset Management. Secondly, after a period of 17 years during which Oxford won 16 times, Cambridge came back with seven wins.

Are the two features related? Yes, but only in part. The sponsorship has enabled both clubs to invest in excellent professional coaching and support, but without affecting the amateur ethos of the contestants. The coaching standards have attracted some of the world's best postgraduate oarsmen and as a consequence of this Oxford and Cambridge have continued to be significant nurseries of internationals, both British and others.

In the period of Oxford dominance from 1976 to 1992 it was fashionable to ascribe the difference entirely to the number of overseas oarsmen in the Oxford ranks, but the statistics show that this is too simplistic an explanation. The proportion rowing for Isis in comparison with Goldie was higher than that in the blue boats, yet Goldie were beating Isis regularly. In the period 1993 to 1999, when Cambridge were winning, the proportion favoured Oxford even more. The explanation lies partly in the collapse of the Cambridge system in the late 1970s, partly in the quality of the incomers, but mostly in concentration on rowing basics by the coaching teams.

In 1976 it was clear from October that Oxford would be a powerful and excellent crew, the heaviest at just over 14 stone average and with the heaviest man, Steve Plunkett, at 16 stone 5lb. They justified their reputation by winning by six and a half lengths in fast conditions, in 16 mins 56 secs, 37 seconds faster than the 1974 time and 36 seconds faster than the Putney to Mortlake record set by Isis only half an hour beforehand.

1 *Colin Moynihan, Oxford cox 1977, getting his weight down at Young's Brewery*

2 *Sue Brown, first female cox, 1981*

3 *Boris Rankov, winner of a record six consecutive races with Oxford from 1978 to 1983*

4 *Women who steered (left to right) Samantha Benham, Carole Burton, Liz Chick, Leigh Weiss, Lisa Ross-Magenty*

84 BATTLE OF THE BLUES

Cambridge win

They could have done a 360 degree turn and looped the loop and they'd have still beaten us

Liz Chick, Oxford cox 1994

In camera *continued*

So through the years the coverage has expanded and become ever more ambitious. But however well it is planned, there are some things you can't control. Somewhere resting at the bottom of the Thames is a BBC camera, literally swept off a boat by a ferocious wind. It is every producer's nightmare that with just minutes to go, your plans are thrown up in the air. In 2000, when the crews were about to take to the water, news came in that the helicopter could not fly because of low cloud. Suddenly I was faced with a situation without radio cameras, boat tracking or on-board cameras, with four and a quarter miles of one of sport's highest profile events to cover. But such moments are part and parcel of the coverage of the boat race. For the television audience it is drama guaranteed: there have been sinkings, crashes, the clashing of oars, a restart, and the tightest finish in 2003.

Perhaps the very special relationship between the viewer and the race is more interesting than advances in coverage and technology. The boat race remains enduringly popular with the audience at home. Why should so many people tune in to what some would consider an anachronism? A remarkable 7.7 million watched the race in 2003 on television, but then the boat race has always attracted impressive audiences. Who can resist the appeal of the true Corinthian spirit of the two crews who devote themselves for months of gruelling training for twenty minutes in the spotlight, their only reward the honour of being a member of the winning crew? Who can forget the television pictures at the end of the race, one crew slumped exhausted and beaten, the other, arms raised elated in triumph?

The feeling amongst the production crew is probably somewhere between the two: a job well done – now for next year.

Brasenose on the Cherwell in 1823, the earliest known print of racing on the Isis

Trail blazing imagery THOMAS E WEIL

The last two centuries have seen explosive growth in personal wealth, leisure time, game sports and entertainment activities, and in the publishing, broadcasting and film industries that depend on and support them. The almost unimaginable attention commanded by the boat race a century ago has been much diluted by the extraordinary variety of choices available to today's spectator or sports enthusiast, but the boat race image endures as an iconic reference to this unique and ancient event.

Choices of how to depict a team sport range from the capture of decisive moments in a contest, to displays of athletic power, grace or emotion, to portraits of teams or individual members. These images are used to report news, to sell products, to glorify teams and stars, or to record history. Today's dominant team sports suit these options in ways that boat racing does not. The story of the early prominence and subsequent eclipse of public boat racing imagery has been influenced by numerous factors, including the nature of the sport as a subject for depiction; the relative bloom and decline of boat racing as a focus of public interest over the last two centuries; and the evolution of the technology for capturing and publishing graphic images. This brief chapter touches upon the scope and variety of printed boat race imagery that has been produced; the larger tale of the virtual disappearance of this imagery remains to be told.

Since 1829, printed scenes of the boat race have served a myriad of purposes and taken innumerable forms. Boat race illustrations have delighted and denigrated, informed and insulted, recorded and ridiculed, and seduced and sold. They have appeared on match boxes, tobacco premium cards and cartes de visite that can fit in a pocket, and on prints, posters and banners that dominate an office or study wall. Boat race views have been placed on mugs, plates, handkerchiefs and two stevengraphs. Rowing scenes are as ubiquitous in nineteenth-century British decorative art as those of any other team sport.

Tuesday's never Bluesday

Tuesday is the only day of the week when there has never been a university boat race. Wednesday has proved the most popular alternative to the regulation Saturday, the most recent Wednesday being in 1937. The first occasion when the race was held on a Sunday was the re-row of 1984, but in 2003 the race was planned for a Sunday for the first time, repeated in 2004.

Commercial sponsorship of the boat race started in 1977 with Ladbrokes. Both crews selected unusual boats, Oxford an early Carbocraft made of composite materials which spelt the end of wooden racing boats, and Cambridge the Imperial College prototype monocoque hull. The gap between the available talent was even more than in the previous year and Oxford won by seven lengths after leading all the way.

Boris Rankov, who was to set a record of six consecutive appearances for Oxford, took part in his first race in 1978. After two consecutive 'processions', this one had more excitement. There was a strong tide and a squally south-west wind. There was a serious battle to Hammersmith bridge, which Oxford reached four seconds ahead. Both crews now ran into very rough conditions and progressed along the Surrey shore with Oxford in the lead and gaining slowly. Staying afloat became the major task in Corney reach. While Cambridge took on water from the crossing before Duke's Meadows, Oxford, who had a cutwater fitted on their boat, managed the conditions better and achieved a ten-second lead by Barnes bridge, shortly after which Cambridge were hit by a squall, swung diagonally across the tide and slowly sank, with Oxford some two lengths ahead, producing some dramatic television pictures.

The 150th anniversary of the first race, 1979, saw Bob Janousek, the GB Olympic coach, in charge at Cambridge, the first time since the 1850s that a non-Oxbridge coach had been involved. His efforts were thwarted on the night before the race when the stroke, John Woodhouse, suffered appendicitis and was out of the boat. Oxford won by three and a half lengths.

1 *The Race by Gustave Doré, illustration of the 1870 Boat Race from London Pilgrimage*

2 *The Finish, 1882, from The Graphic*

That's the end of my career as a Trivial Pursuit question.

John Pritchard, Cambridge winner in 1986 after Cambridge won again in 1993

Trail blazing imagery *continued*

The printed imagery of the Oxford-Cambridge race is as old as the rivalry itself. A small undated engraving by William Havell of the initial race, held at Henley in 1829, and a larger aquatint of the 1829 Oxford eight on its home waters, are two of the earliest such prints known. The British sporting art tradition has long focussed on animals, but, at its fringes, cricket and boat racing, the first two team sports, found a place in the decorative arts corpus, and many of the early boat-race aquatints, etchings and lithographs are rare, attractive and valuable pieces produced by masters of the print-making art.

Beginning with the first great boat racing print, Havell's view of an 1822 contest on the Isis, printmakers produced extraordinary scenes of boats and boat racing at Oxford, at Cambridge, at Henley and on the tideway. Major decorative prints of the boat race were not issued frequently, and most date from 40 years or more after the start of the rivalry.

Smaller fine Boat Race views include steel engravings from 1841 and 1865. Prominent among the larger prints are a rare untitled 1850s lithograph of eights racing along the then rural course from Putney to Mortlake; the 1868 lithograph by Hogarth, vividly depicting the chaos before the authorities began regulating river traffic; Beckmann's c.1870 view from a cluster of spectator skiffs; the classic 1871 lithograph by Lipschitz, notable for its depiction of starboard stroked eights and the divided attention of the spectators; the 1877 dead heat by Robinson; Sherburn's 1880s etching of the race passing Crabtree Wharf; and two chromo- or oleographs of the last two decades of the nineteenth century (each paired with a Henley regatta view). More recently, boat racing has been the subject of noted artists such as Julian Trevelyan, Annabel Eyres and Vorticists Sybil Andrews and Cyril Power. The rivalry itself aside, landmarks on the course have been portrayed by innumerable artists and photographers, from Farington to Whistler to Taunt.

BATTLE OF THE BLUES

1980 produced one of the close races of the Oxford winning period. Cambridge had a very good Etonian in their crew who was to get greater fame as an actor and comedian – Hugh Laurie, son of a previous Cambridge president, Ran Laurie. It was a reasonably tight race all the way to Barnes bridge, where Oxford were five seconds ahead. Shortly after this the nineteen-year-old Oxford bow, Stephen Francis, collapsed and took no further part. It subsequently emerged that he was ill with hepatitis. The seven Oxford men just managed to hold off a push by Cambridge to win by a canvas.

The Oxford crew of 1981 was regarded as vintage, but the year will be best remembered as that in which a woman first gained a blue – Sue Brown, the dark blues' cox. Oxford made it a procession from the mile onwards and won by eight lengths. This was the first time that Oxford had won by that margin since 1878. The 1982 race was closer, often attributed to a more rigorous training programme instituted by the Cambridge president Roger Stephens. Nevertheless Oxford won by three and a quarter lengths. 1983 saw the eighth successive Oxford victory and Rankov's sixth, the most blues ever won by any oarsman of either university. Despite gastric upsets, Oxford won by four and a half lengths.

The 1984 race was another unusual one, but for all the wrong reasons. About 20 minutes before the start of the race, Cambridge, coxed by Peter Hobson, were practising a start below the stakeboats and totally failed to see a barge moored in the middle of the river, crashed into it and snapped off the bow section, writing off the boat. Next day Oxford went clear by Harrods and rowed on to win by three and three-quarter lengths in a new record of 16 mins 45 secs.

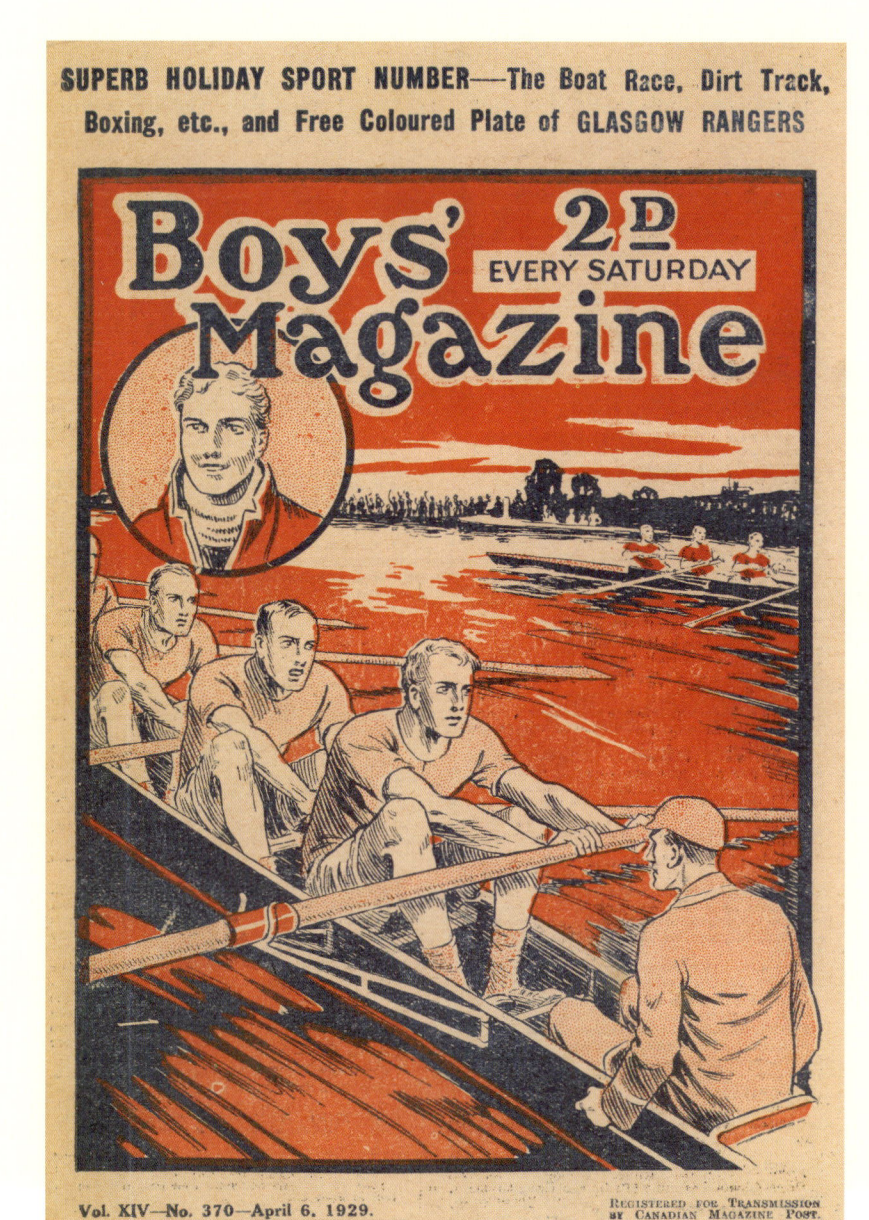

Foul deeds at Barnes

We tussled for the line to Barnes Bridge. We could hear each other's coxes. The umpire's warnings, at first to both crews, compounding my distraction. Then the warnings were directed at Isis, ahead by three men; blades clashing, water splashing.

Somebody put the brakes on. It's like we've dropped anchor. The helicopter shots show a blade clash between their seven and our four, and a second clash with our two whose oar springs from its gate and his grip, rotating on the speeding water in an astonishing vertical arc,

before he dexterously catches it, and tries to replace the button in its gate. But the pin on the gate has sheared. Our craft is broken. There's no continuing. As the red flag is waved, Bracey our cox raises his arm to the umpire to appeal. We collapse and stop amidst breathless expletives.

Eventually the megaphone rings out. 'Isis, for damage caused outside of your rightful water, you are disqualified. Goldie wins,' announces umpire John Garrett.

Dobs Vye, Goldie stroke, on Isis being disqualified, 1990

1 Oxford's boathouse on the Isis, 1913

2 Oxford's boathouse burned down, 1999

3 Boys Magazine, 1929

Trail blazing imagery *continued*

One explanation for the paucity of Boat Race prints in the decorative arts may have been the surfeit of such views in the popular press of the nineteenth century. Notwithstanding the rise of numerous competing game sport activities towards the end of the century, images of boat racing provide the dominant sports team visual experience in the popular media of the period. While rowing imagery might appear in the illustrated news weeklies at any time of the year, views of the boat race and Henley regatta dominated.

Of these, the boat race stood supreme, often monopolizing the covers and full and double page illustrations for the issues preceding and following the contest. At the height of the rivalry's popularity, the Graphic published 'The Spurt' (1878) and 'Are You Ready?' (1879), two enormous boat race supplements which remain among the iconic images of the contest. The number and content of these wood engravings by the leading illustrators of the day provide a finely tuned measure of public interest in the event, and, as the principal journals of the ilk and era, the Graphic, the Illustrated London News, and the Illustrated Sporting and Dramatic News offer fruitful fields for further study.

These wood engravings, the most common and affordable of older boat race views, also reflect more clearly than any other body of graphic work the peculiar challenges of depicting rowing contests. As the boat race often becomes a procession, the event rarely gives rise to the dramatic moments that enliven most game sports. The distance of the artists and the spectators from the boats denies them a view of the agony and ecstasy of the rowers, and, for most viewers, only a few moments of the race are distantly visible.

But the boat race has never been only about boat racing, and this is demonstrated more clearly in the popular magazine illustrations of the contest than anywhere else. Each year, preceding the race, there would frequently be one or more portraits of the rival crews, in group poses or in individual views, and there would often be images of the crews at practice, putting their boats in the water, fixing their stretchers, taking their time trials, carrying their boats to the boathouse, or off for a training walk or run.

BATTLE OF THE BLUES 91

The 1985 race was notable for the battle of the coxes – Henrietta Shaw for Cambridge and Seth Lessor for Oxford – in a level race to Chiswick eyot. Then the dark blues made a spurt which Cambridge could not answer and moved ahead to win by four and three-quarter lengths. This was a record tenth consecutive win for Oxford.

The rowing year culminating in the 1986 race dawned brighter for Cambridge than any of the previous ten. The light blues took charge from the first stroke and won by seven lengths to break the Oxford winning spell. The 1987 race was the first sponsored by Beefeater Gin, a company with long associations with the race through its chairman Alan Burrough, and Alan Mays-Smith, both of whom had been Cambridge oarsmen and London representatives of the boat race.

Losing after such a long run caused trauma at Oxford. Before the 1987 race many of the squad mutinied against president Donald Macdonald and coach Dan Topolski. Five Americans eventually refused to row, leaving a blue boat that was thought to have no chance. The weather appeared to enjoy the drama, for in squally conditions, a Wagnerian lightning strike took out the BBC commentary just before the start. The ensuing race was won by good tactics by Oxford who, on Middlesex, headed directly for shelter under the Fulham wall leaving Cambridge to battle through rough water. Cambridge did not recover the lead that Oxford gained, and the dark blues won by four lengths, the start of another winning streak.

Cambridge practise on the Ouse at Ely

92 BATTLE OF THE BLUES

BOAT RACE RECORD TIME: **CAMBRIDGE 1998**

MILE POST	HAMMERSMITH BRIDGE	CHISWICK STEPS	BARNES BRIDGE	RACE FINISH
3.33 minutes	**6.20** minutes	**9.56** minutes	**13.32** minutes	**16.19** minutes

Trail blazing imagery   *continued*

In the week of the race the images tend to concentrate on the spectators, of all classes, whether observing the weather as they prepare to leave home, or jostling at railway stations en route, or sitting on terraces or in carriages on the river banks, or squeezed into boats along the course, or jammed into steamers following the race, or crowding bridges over the river, or perched in trees. Many in attendance are depicted as more intent on one another than the contest – they picnic, or fall in love, or purchase ribbons, or listen to minstrels, or trip on the towpath or slip off the bank or tumble out of boats. They are young and old, university men, drunkards, policemen, pickpockets, vendors, entertainers, lords and ladies, and boatmen and bargees. The story is the unique gathering, without ticket or exclusion, for a few hours on one spring day along four miles of river in one of the major capitals of the world, of every sort of citizen of the metropolis, brought together on the occasion of the boat race, and these images tell it well and joyfully.

The week after the contest, the result is the news, usually conveyed with as little excitement as accompanies the finish of most races. 'Oxford [or Cambridge] won by so many lengths.' Here is a picture, perhaps of the start or at an early point when the outcome was still in doubt, or here is the procession, the victor close to the observer, the vanquished boat at some distance. There are few images of the losing crew after the race.

Boat Race images appeared with steadfast regularity in the weekly news magazines, especially in the Illustrated London News, from the 1840s through the 1960s. Wood engravings gave way to photogravures in the late 1880s, then to photographs by the turn of the century, but the press of other news and the speed with which illustrations could be published reduced the coverage of the contest to one or two pages in one or two issues a year, focusing on the competitors and an action shot or two. After the first world war the event was rarely covered as the unique public occasion it had been for the preceding half century.

The 1988 Oxford crew was a powerful one under the presidency of the American Olympic oarsman Chris Penny, a mutineer from the year before. While Topolski stood down as coach after the 1987 problems, OUBC hired Steve Royle as their first managing coach and Penny engaged the British Olympic coach Mike Spracklen as chief coach. Many of the mutineers' reforms were put in place, and the new Oxford won by five and a half lengths after a delayed start to replace their six man's broken stretcher.

As the races became more closely fought, the coxing became more competitive, particularly when seeking the stream in the first few minutes, and the 1989 race followed this pattern. Whether the coxes would have benefited more from holding their own station and avoiding the blade clashes is a moot point. The race was close to Chiswick reach, and even here Oxford only moved slowly ahead to win by two and a half lengths.

In 1990, with Jonny Searle as president, Oxford featured an oarsman of outstanding talent in Matt Pinsent and the heaviest crew to date at average of just under 15 stone, almost two stone a man heavier than their rivals. The fact that Cambridge held them over much of the course was due to the fighting qualities of the light blue stroke Adam Wright, who refused to be intimidated.

The Oxford crew in 1991 was one of the lightest for several years but was still some nine and a half pounds per man heavier than Cambridge and had far more experience, with internationals Pinsent and Rupert Obholzer. Cambridge were beginning to show again the technical skill of the past. But experience and power overcame technique and the dark blues won by four and a quarter lengths in 16 mins 59 secs, the third time that 17 minutes had been bettered.

In 1992, an Olympic year, there were no outstanding internationals in either crew. Oxford had a young but good stroke in Ian Gardiner and in large measure it was his drive around the outside of the Surrey bend which enabled them to win by one and a quarter lengths. This took Oxford to 16 wins out of 17 races, with only one more required to level the series at 69 each, with one dead-heat.

Oxford, with four Olympians came to the start as firm favourites in 1993, while Cambridge were an unknown quantity, having, for the first time, spent the first of the last two weeks before the race practising in Nottingham instead of at Putney. Cambridge were using new asymmetrical 'cleaver' blades, but Oxford rejected them on the basis of insufficient experience of their use in possibly severe weather conditions. It was a great surprise when Cambridge not only pulled away to a lead of half a length by the end of the Fulham wall, but extended it to three and a half lengths at the finish. The answer to the question 'would this be a one-off win for Cambridge again?' was answered in 1994 when a light blue crew which included two German world champions, Peter Höltzenbein and Thorsten Streppelhoff, accomplished a six and a half length win.

Cambridge return from practice, 1870

Presidents who miss

In 1996 John Carver became the sixth Cambridge president to miss the race when he was excluded following two unsuccessful wrist operations for tenosynovitis. Carver rowed for Goldie in 1994 but never got a blue, although he was an outstanding leader on the bank in 1996. Of oarsmen who miss their chance of a blue, most do so because of illness, but a few presidents have de-selected themselves. Cambridge's Quintus Travis was not picked when president in 1986 and, like Carver, never got a blue after rowing for Goldie in 1984 and 1985. The 1986 blue boat ended Oxford's ten-year winning streak. Sixteen Oxford presidents have not rowed, the most recent being Ed Bellamy who was in the blue boat in 1996 but was relegated to Isis in his presidential year of 1997. Sam McLennan becomes the seventeenth in 2004, out because of a back injury.

Trail blazing imagery *continued*

Two magazines that commented on London life for decades are also dependable sources of boat race imagery. Some of the most amusing insights on the event (and the reactions to it of an often puzzled public) appeared in cartoons in the humour magazine Punch, while the society weekly Vanity Fair typically found space in at least one issue a year for a 'Men of the Day' caricature that related to the Oxford-Cambridge boat race rivalry.

Photographs relating to the boat race offer a fascinating alternative to engravings and other illustrations, and they may be classed in two general categories: wire photos used for news purposes from the 1920s to 1950s (and available to collectors today as photo libraries are sold off), and commercially published photographs, including, in general chronological order, cartes de visite, cabinet cards, album plates and stereoviews for sale to oarsmen, their families, or the public, cigarette premium cards, and postcards.

While no in-depth study of printed boat race imagery has yet been written, some of the earlier books that contain a number of boat race illustrations include London – A Pilgrimage (1872), illustrated by Gustave Doré, which includes a chapter on the boat race with one of the most telling views of the event; Drinkwater and Sanders's University Boat Race Official Centenary History 1829-1929; and A Lloyd-Taylor's catalogue of the collection of rowing pictures and trophies at the Coach and Eight (1953).

The commercial world has not been shy in using boat race images or references when it has suited. One of the most striking large boat race lithographs is an advertising poster featuring a woman in vivid blue watching the race, and, long before the advent of commercial sponsorship, Cadbury's, Dunlop Tyres, Hamilton Watch, and the Morris car company used boat race scenes to promote their products. Tobacco companies also used rowing subjects extensively on the premium cards which they included in their cigarette packets. The Ogden's cards of the 1900s tended to show eights in the water, while the 1930s Gallaher and Hill brand cards also displayed such Blues as T G Askwith, J R Bingham, T A Brocklebank, R W G Holdsworth, T Frame-Thomson and A B Sanford.

From the late 1980s both universities, supported by the sponsorship, concentrated on professional coaches of international status, with Mark Lees and John Wilson initially going to Oxford and then moving to Cambridge, and Sean Bowden reversing the direction. At the same time squad rowing became more of an all-year commitment. Cambridge further strengthened their coaching team in 1995 by taking on Robin Williams as chief coach and inviting Harry Mahon, the New Zealand 'guru', to act as their finishing coach, while Topolski was brought back into the Oxford team.

In 1995, after a close race for two miles, Cambridge pulled ahead at Chiswick reach and went on to win by four lengths. Since then, up to 2003, the crews have not been separated by more than a length at Hammersmith. Gone, for the present, are the processions. In 1996, with the two university chancellors – the Duke of Edinburgh in the Cambridge launch and Lord Jenkins in the Oxford one – following the race, Cambridge again won, by two and three-quarter lengths. The last week of practice for the 1997 was undertaken in sinking winds and a very uncomfortable race appeared likely, but on Saturday the wind abated. It was a close-fought race with a substantial number of warnings, mainly against Cambridge, all the way to Hammersmith bridge, where Oxford were one second ahead. Then Cambridge held their rivals round the outside of the bend and drew level at Chiswick steps, going ahead along Duke's meadows with the bend in their favour to win by two lengths.

Just as Oxford had outstanding crews in the 1970s and 1980s, so 1998 provided such a crew for the light blues in the year which was to become the last of the Beefeater sponsorship. The Cambridge crew was the heaviest (at 14 stone 13lb average), the tallest (at 6 ft 5 $\frac{1}{2}$ ins average) and after a close race over a substantial part of the course, they went on to win by three lengths in the record time of 16 mins 19 secs. This reduced the 1984 Oxford record by 26 seconds.

The Finish in 1846, when the race was rowed from Mortlake to Putney. This was the first use of out-rigged boats

Olympians and women too

The Boat Race has been a breeding ground for countless international oarsmen, including Olympic and world champions for several nations. In recent years it has also attracted oarsmen who have gained international honours before coming to Oxford or Cambridge. It has also influenced the development of other boat races such as the Harvard versus Yale match (1852), which introduced inter-collegiate sport to America. It has spawned several imitations, the most notable being the Oxford and Cambridge women's race. The first of these was in 1927, marked for style rather than judged for speed. The present series began in 1975 over 2000 metres at Henley-on-Thames, which by 2003 Cambridge led by 38 wins to Oxford's 20. There are also women's reserve crew races between Osiris (Oxford) and Blondie, men's and women's lightweight boat races, and a men's lightweight reserves race between Granta (Cambridge) and Nepthys.

Trail blazing imagery *continued*

In the 'all things great and small' classes, postcards and posters provide intriguing extremes in printed boat race imagery. So-called 'real photo' postcards of the rival crews were produced in significant quantities almost every year from 1900 through the 1930s, and, whether showing the crews posed for team portraits or seated in their boats at Putney, they provide a valuable record of the period. Though typically pedestrian in conception and execution, boat race postcards are relatively easily found, and what a delight if one discovers that the accompanying message relates to the crew or the race!

Conversely, the early boat race posters published by London Transport in the 1920s and 1930s constitute at once some of the greatest rarities of the species and some of the most attractive. Issued in striking colors to catch the attention of London commuters, the biggest of the class were not generally available for sale, and, as quintessential ephemera, may be the highlight of any collection. The smaller posters, made as placards for trains or buses, are also attractive and are almost as rare.

Taken as a whole, printed boat race imagery occupies a modest place in the annals of fine and decorative art. In the depiction of the development of modern team sport, however, and of one of its greatest traditions, this body of work has never been rivalled.

1976–2003

In 1999 Aberdeen Asset Management became sponsors. The average height rose further by three-quarters of an inch and Josh West (Cambridge) at 6ft 5½ins became the tallest oarsman. The race to Hammersmith was even, but the light blues on Surrey moved away in Chiswick reach to win by three and a half lengths in the second fastest time ever (16 mins 41 secs).

The first fourteen minutes of the race in 2000 was rowed side by side despite uncomfortable conditions leaving two very tired looking crews to fight out the final stretch. Oxford, on the inside of the final bend, moved into the lead just before Barnes bridge, winning by three lengths. In 2001 a similar side-by-side tussle was not to be. Along the boathouse reach at Putney, the two coxes tangled for position and after several warnings, mainly against Cambridge, the Cambridge bow's blade was dislodged from his hands in a clash just after Oxford, in the lead by several feet, had received a warning. The umpire, Rupert Obholzer, stopped the race and restarted it. Oxford never recovered from what many believed was an unfair decision, and Cambridge held a modest lead to Chiswick reach before striding on to win by two and a half lengths.

There then followed two races which rival those of 1949 and 1952 as the most exciting to date. Oxford won in 2002 by three quarters of a length and 2003 by only one foot. Both were fought side-by-side over nearly all the way, with the crews alternately fractionally ahead. The result should probably be ascribed in both races to the excellent stroking of Oxford's Matt Smith, though he had a little assistance in 2002 when Cambridge's Seb Mayer was in trouble from Duke's meadows.

Two great races by great crews, with great physique and tenacity and a great tribute to the University Boat Race as it approaches its 150th race in its 175th year. The score stands at Oxford 71, Cambridge 77 with one dead-heat.

1 *Oxford celebrate, 2003*

2 *Opposing brothers, 2003. Left to right: Matt Smith (Oxford), Ben Smith (Cambridge), James Livingston (Cambridge), Dave Livingston (Oxford)*

3 *Steve Rider of BBC Grandstand with the presidents at the toss for Stations, 2001*

Oxford win by one foot

The Boat Race is such a wonderful race in terms of the sheer number of variables that enter into it, such as the umpire and stream and the tide and the bends. There's no buoys between the crews, you could have a clash, there's so many things that could happen.

Acer Nethercott,
Oxford's cox 2003

To have four old boys actually rowing in the Boat Race and to have two sets of brothers each on opposite sides is really the stuff that dreams are made of. It's a wonderful day and a wonderful achievement for the boys, the families, the school, and all the rowing coaches at school and beyond who have brought them to the standard they are at.

Barry Martin,
headmaster of Hampton School 2003

This was a great event for the sport of rowing, which ultimately we are ambassadors of.

Tim Wooge,
Cambridge stroke and president 2003

Oxford win by one foot, 2003

Blues from 1946 to 2003

OXFORD

Adams J F Eton College and University 2002 (I-G), 2003
Andrews M D Abingdon School and Magdalen 1980, 1981
Angier P D P Westminster School and Christ Church 1973
Arundel R L Marlborough College and Merton 1948, 1949
Ayer T H MIT USA and Worcester 1997 (I-G), 1998 (I-G), 1999, 2000
Badcock F D M Harrow School and Christ Church 1958
Baines M G C T Eton College and Keble 1972
Baird A G H Radley College and Christ Church 1974 (I-G), 1975, 1976
Barnard P F Eton College and Christ Church 1957
Barrett R St. Edward's School and Pembroke 1956, 1957
Barry J M Dulwich College and Queen's 1946
Barry T C M Radley College and Oriel 1978 (I-G), 1979 (I-G), 1980
Bate R C I Tonbridge School and St. Edmund Hall 1960, 1961
Beak D R H Radley College and Oriel 1975, 1976
Bellamy E J Durham University and Keble 1996, 1997 (I-G)
Benham Samantha L St. Mary's School Calne and Brasenose 1993
Berger P A University of Pennsylvania USA and Lincoln 1996, 1998
Berners-Lee C P Emanuel School London and Wadham 1978 (I-G), 1979
Bevan N V Shrewsbury School and Balliol 1963
Blacker J G C Eton College and Balliol 1950
Blackwall C I Radley College and Keble 1966 (I-G), 1967
Blanchard G B King's College School London and Oriel 1989
Bland J L King Edward VI School Stafford and Merton 1978 (I-G), 1980, 1981, 1983
Blanda R University of Washington USA and Brasenose 1997
Bockstoce J R Yale University USA and St. Edmund Hall 1967, 1968
Bolshaw K The King's School Chester and Christ Church 1971, 1972
Bonham M F Radley College and Oriel 2000 (I-G), 2001
Bourne R M A Eton College and New College 1946, 1947
Bourne-Taylor R E G Abingdon School and Christ Church 2001, 2002, 2003
Bray D G St. Edward's School and Keble 1964
Bridge P A J Eton College and Oriel 1991, 1992
Brodie P N Oundle School and Oriel 1946, 1947, 1948
Brown K C Cornell University USA and Christ Church 1976
Brown Susan Taunton School and Wadham 1981, 1982
Burch B J Cheltenham College and Pembroke 1999 (I-G), 2000, 2001, 2002
Burnell P C D Eton College and Magdalen 1962

Byatt R A Gordonstoun School and New College 1953
Cadoux-Hudson T A D St. Mary's Hospital London and New College 1987, 1988
Callender D N Eton College and Trinity 1950, 1951
Calvert A T University of Tasmania and New College 1968, (I-G), 1969, 1970
Calvert J N Thirsk School and St. Edmund Hall 1974 (I-G), 1975, 1976
Carnegie R H Melbourne University Australia and New College 1956, 1957
Carr F C Eton College and Keble 1965 (I-G), 1966
Carstairs J R L St. Edward's School and Christ Church 1946
Cartledge G J Hampton School and New College 1984 (I-G), 1985
Carver G A Yale University USA and Balliol 1951
Cavenagh A J M Winchester College and Magdalen 1949, 1950
Chapman Abbie C Lady Eleanor Holles School and St. Hilda's 1995
Chester J R Monkton Combe School and Keble 1960, 1961
Cheveley R G C Tonbridge School and Pembroke 1988 (I-G),1989
Chick H Elizabeth Helsby High School and Christ Church 1992, 1994
Chugani N Hampton School and St. Catherine's 1990 (I-G), 1991
Clark C G H California State University USA and University 1986
Clay H E Eton College and Magdalen 1981 (I-G), 1982, 1983
Clay J M Eton College and Magdalen 1949, 1950
Clay R C Eton College and New College 1981 (I-G), 1982, 1984, 1987 (I-G)
Clegg D R H University College London and Keble 1994, 1995, 1996
Clegg R D Tiffin School and St. Edmund Hall 1965, 1966
Conington N A Hampton School and Oriel 1980, 1981, 1982
Coode E R University of Newcastle and Keble 1998
Cooper G V Eton College and Keble 1961
Corroon H S Monash University Australia and Keble 1995
Cox D W A Bryanston College and St. Peter's 1964
Crawford J R Winchester College and Pembroke 1977 (I-G), 1978, 1979
Crockford R A Prince Henry's School Evesham and Corpus Christi 1977 (I-G), 1978, 1979
Crooks M A L Princeton University USA and St. Anne's 1999
Cross D A Winchester College and Balliol 1956
Crotty M M Princeton University USA and Keble 1999
Dale F J L Emanuel School, London, and Keble 1969, 1970, 1971
Dart J K G Radley College and Christ Church 1969 (I-G), 1970
Davenport D T H Radley College and University 1953
Davidge C G V Eton College and Trinity 1949, 1951, 1952
Davis C M Eton College and Lincoln 1960, 1961, 1962
Davy S G Eton College and Worcester 1991 (I-G), 1992

Dillon T G King's College London and Oriel 1989
Diserens M J Wallingford School and Keble 1979, 1980
Dixon B G Bedford School and Pembroke 2002, 2003
Douglas-Mann S C H Westminster School and St. Edmund Hall 1959
Ducker J H Monkton Combe School and St. Edmund Hall 1958
Duncan J M Shrewsbury School and Keble 1967 (I-G), 1968 (I-G), 1969
Dunn A G G Eton College and Lincoln 2000, 2001 (I-G), 2002
Dunstan M R St. Olave's School and Worcester 1984 (I-G), 1986
Eastman M T Radley College and Christ Church 1970 (I-G), 1971
Ebsworth-Snow R E Bradfield School and Magdalen 1946
Edwards A D The King's School Worcester and St. Peter's 1975 (I-G), 1976
Edwards D C R Downside School and Christ Church 1958, 1959
Eggenkamp G Delft University of Technology, Netherlands, and Keble 2002
Elliott I L Canford School and Keble 1960, 1961
Emerton R P Abingdon School and Christ Church 1980 (I-G), 1981
Evans J M Princeton University USA and University 1983, 1984
Evans W M Queen's University Canada and University 1983, 1984
Fage J L Wrekin College and St. Edmund Hall 1958, 1959
Fail J Bedford Modern School and Oriel 1976 (I-G), 1978
Faulkner R G B Radley College and Trinity 1948
Fink W R Yale University USA and Keble 1965, 1968
Fishlock R L S The King's School Canterbury and St. Edmund Hall 1960
Fisk G C Geelong Grammar School Australia and Oriel 1948, 1949, 1950
Foster S J L Brentwood School and Pembroke 1981 (I-G), 1982
Foster T J C University of London and St. Cross 1997
Francis S R W St. Paul's School London and Corpus Christi 1980, 1982 (I-G)
Frandsen S University of California Berkeley USA and St. Edmund Hall 2003
Freeman C H The King's School Canterbury, and Keble 1966, 1967
Freeman R A D The King's School Canterbury, and Magdalen 1966
Frost A R A Eton College and Oriel 1996
Gaffney M US Naval Academy USA and Hertford 1988, 1989, 1990
Gardiner I W The Glasgow Academy and St. Peter's 1992, 1993
Gee K B Hampton School and Worcester 1969
Gee R J D University of Tasmania and St. John's 1968 (I-G), 1970
Gish P A Dartmouth College USA and Oriel 1987
Gladstone P Eton College and Christ Church 1950, 1952
Gleave J R W Uppingham School and Magdalen 1946, 1947, 1948
Gleeson P F St. Martin's School Brentwood and Hertford 1987, 1988, 1988

OXFORD BLUES FROM 1946 TO 2003 *continued*

Glynne-Jones D R Magdalen College School Oxford and Jesus *1952*
Gobbo J A Melbourne University Australia and Magdalen *1954, 1955*
Gomm C P M Cheltenham College and Balliol *1961*
Gordon-Brown A S University of Cape Town South Africa and Keble *1993 (I-G), 1994*
Greaney P A Abingdon School and St. Edmund Hall *1995 (I-G), 1996 (I-G), 1997, 1998*
Green A S Haberdashers Aske's School and Christ Church *1986*
Grubor L Imperial College London and Somerville *1997*
Hackworth P E P St. Paul's School London and Oriel *2001 (I-G), 2002*
Hall A J Hampton School and Keble *1970, 1971, 1972, 1973*
Hall M J W Winchester College and Lincoln *1958*
Hammond E C B Clifton College and Brasenose *1953*
Hammond J F Harvard University USA and New College *1996*
Hare P M St. Alban's School and Balliol *1983 (I-G), 1984 (I-G), 1985*
Harris M G C St. Edward's School and Oriel *1973 (I-G), 1974 (I-G), 1975*
Harrison J J H Shrewsbury School and Trinity *1954*
Hawkes M J Bedford School and New College *1951*
Hawksley J P W Emanuel School London and Balliol *1968, 1971, 1972*
Hayes J Shrewsbury School and New College *1950*
Head P J Hampton School and Oriel *1978 (I-G), 1979, 1981*
Heathcote C J Allhallows School and Jesus *1989 (I-G), 1990*
Hecht J H E Universitaet Bochum Hagen Goettingen Germany and Keble *1998*
Higgins S E Kent School USA and Exeter *1981 (I-G), 1983*
Higgs D M Oxted County School and Balliol *1969, 1970*
Hinchliffe J E C The King's School Canterbury and Trinity *1950*
Holland G R N Radley College and Oriel *1980 (I-G), 1982*
Howard R L Shrewsbury School and Worcester *1957, 1959*
Howell Jnr H W Yale University USA and St. Edmund Hall *1965*
Howick J W London School of Economics and Keble *1996*
Howles J S The Royal Grammar School Newcastle and University *1953*
Hull R A Robinson College Cambridge and Oriel *1987, 1988, 1990*
Hume H P M Yale University USA and Pembroke *1991, 1992*
Humphreys C P A Hampton School and Oriel *1996 (I-G), 1997, 1998, 1999*
Hunt S D Radley College and Keble *1971, 1972 (I-G)*
Hutchings J E University of Manitoba Canada and Christ Church *1974 (I-G), 1975*
Innes G S Pangbourne College and Oriel *1974, 1975, 1976*
Irving J Yale University USA and Keble *1997*
Irving S G Magdalen College School Oxford and Keble *1971 (I-G), 1972 (I-G), 1973*
Jamison D G Radley College and Magdalen *1947*
Jensen J E Yale University USA and New College *1967*
Jones G R D University of Sydney Australia and New College *1983, 1984, 1985, 1986*

Kawaja J R W Princeton University USA and St. Catherine's *1995*
Keniston K H Harvard University USA and Balliol *1952*
Kennard M S Radley College and St. Edmund Hall *1965 (I-G), 1966, 1967, 1968*
Kirkpatrick A K Methodist College Belfast and Oriel *1982*
Kristol T B Harvard University USA and Oriel *1996*
Lander J R H Shrewsbury School and Christ Church *1959*
Lang W J Wallingford Grammar School and Magdalen *1983, 1984, 1985*
Leckie W J H The Edinburgh Academy and Brasenose *1949*
Leigh M J Eton College and Keble *1964, 1965*
Leigh-Wood J Eton College and Keble *1964*
Lesser S R Princeton University USA and Magdalen *1984, 1985*
Lilledahl E B Yale University USA and Nuffield *2000, 2001*
Lindsay A J R Eton College and Brasenose *1997, 1998, 1999*
Lindsay A T Eton College and Magdalen *1959, 1960*
Livingston, D. A., Hampton School and Christ Church *2002 (I-G), 2003*
Livingstone G A University of California Berkeley USA and Oriel *1986*
Lobbenberg A D Shrewsbury School and Balliol *1986 (I-G), 1987, 1988*
Long C L B St. Paul's School London and Oriel *1982 (I-G), 1983 (I-G), 1984*
Lonsdale W R C Monkton Combe School and Keble *1968 (I-G), 1969, 1970*
Lorgen Sn Massachusetts Institute of Technology USA and Nuffield *1994*
Lorgen Sv Harvard University USA and University *1994*
Macdonald D H M Morrison's Academy and Mansfield *1985 (I-G), 1986, 1987*
Mackay D A M Owen's School and Lincoln *1947*
MacLennan C A King Edward VI Camp Hill and Green *1988 (I-G), 1989, 1990 (I-G), 1991, 1992*
MacMillan H J Eton College and Worcester *1994*
Magarey M R Adelaide University Australia and Magdalen *1972, 1973*
Mahne C N Eton College and St. Catherine's *1994*
Mahoney C J Hampton School and Oriel *1979, 1980, 1981*
Mann B Yale University USA and Keble *1996*
Manners R H Winchester College and Brasenose *1993*
Marsden P J Monmouth School and Lincoln *1972 (I-G), 1973 (I-G), 1974*
Marsh W R St. Edward's School and University *1953, 1954*
Martin R W Durham Johnston Comprehensive and University *1990 (I-G), 1991*
Mason E K L King's College School London and Queen's *1956, 1957*
Mason R S Eton College and Keble *1975, 1976, 1977*
Matheson H P Eton College and Keble *1969*
Mathews P H St. Edward's School and St. Edmund Hall *1947*
Mavra B Imperial College London and Jesus *1992, 1993, 1995*
Mawer B S Epsom College and Merton *1956*

McGee L W Brown University USA and Oriel *2002*
McLanahan J B Yale University USA and Pembroke *1993 (I-G), 1994 (I-G), 1995*
McLaren A Kajsa The King's School Canterbury and Pembroke *1999 (I-G), 2000*
McLennan S University of Wisconsin USA and Corpus Christi *2003*
McLeod J G Sydney University Australia and New College *1954, 1955, 1956*
Mead J S St. Edward's School and St. Edmund Hall *1979 (I-G),1980*
Mead R C T Eton College and Keble *1963, 1964*
Meyer E C Canford School and University *1965 (I-G), 1966*
Michelmore A G Melbourne University Australia and New College *1977, 1978*
Michels J G La Salle University USA and Pembroke *1991, 1992, 1993, 1994*
Miller P D The King's School Canterbury and St. Catherine's *1966 (I-G), 1967*
Miller III D J Syracuse University USA and University *1990*
Milling C D Radley College and Merton *1952*
Mills D J The King's School Canterbury and St. Edmund Hall *1965*
Miskin S F A St. Paul's School London and University *1957, 1958*
Moncreiffe Hon P D E M Eton College and Christ Church *1972*
Moncrieff J C St. Edward's School and Christ Church *2001*
Money-Coutts C J A N Eton College and Keble *1975, 1977*
Moore R J Tiffin School and St. Edmund Hall *1977 (I-G), 1978 (I-G), 1979*
Moran M M University of British Columbia Canada and Keble *1977, 1978*
Morland M Q Radley College and Lincoln *1963, 1964, 1965*
Morris G E Bedford School and Oriel *1973 (I-G), 1974*
Morris H J R Radley College and Magdalen *2002 (I-G), 2003*
Morris S R Radley College and St. Edmund Hall *1963, 1965*
Morton Maskell R A Bryanston School and Keble *1962, 1963*
Moynihan C B Monmouth School and University *1975 (I-G), 1977*
Mullard J K Radley College and Keble *1965 (I-G), 1966, 1967*
Nethercott A G The Broxbourne School and University *2002 (I-G), 2003*
Nevin S D Westminster School and Christ Church *1971, 1972 (I-G), 1974*
Nilsson L H K University of Lund Sweden and Hertford *1998, 1999*
Noel R A Oundle School and Christ Church *1948*
Norrish Alison R M Kingston College of Further Education and University *1989*
Obholzer R J Hampton School and St. Catherine's *1990, 1991*
O'Donnell N J Rutgers University USA and Keble *1998 (I-G), 1999*
Ollivant J S Eton College and Worcester *1973*
Pain E O G Sydney University Australia and Lincoln *1954, 1955*
Paine N The King's School Canterbury and Trinity *1956*
Painter A W Shrewsbury School and Hertford *1968*
Palgrave-Brown A Shrewsbury School and Queen's *1947, 1949*
Palm B T Dartmouth College USA and Linacre *2001*

OXFORD BLUES FROM 1946 TO 2003 *continued*

Parish C R W Eton College and Christ Church *1970 (I-G), 1969 (I-G), 1971*
Payne D R Hampton School and Balliol *1972, 1973, 1974*
Pelham H St. Edward's School and Christ Church *1986 (I-G), 1987, 1988*
Penny C G Princeton University USA and St. John's *1988*
Perkins D B Dartmouth College USA and Brasenose *2002*
Philp B M Bryanston School and Worcester *1985, 1986*
Pinsent M C Eton College and St. Catherine's *1990, 1991, 1993*
Plunkett S G H Methodist College Belfast and Queen's *1974 (I-G), 1975 (I-G), 1976*
Poole K K Magdalen College School Oxford and St. John's *1990 (I-G), 1992, 1993, 1994*
Prichard P C Winchester College and New College *1966 (I-G), 1967 (I-G), 1968*
Purssell A J R Oundle School and Oriel *1946, 1947, 1948*
Quick H M C Shrewsbury School and Merton *1952, 1953, 1954*
Raikes R D T Radley College and Merton *1954, 1955*
Raikes R M T Radley College and Trinity *1946*
Raikes T D Radley College and Trinity *1947, 1949*
Rankov N B Bradford Grammar School and St. Hugh's *1974 (I-G), 1975(I-G), 1978, 1979, 1980, 1981, 1982, 1983*
Reed L S T Princeton University USA and St. Catherine's *1995*
Reid A M Yale University USA and Lincoln *2000*
Reininger F M University of Pennsylvania USA and University *1985*
Rendel D D Magdalen College School Oxford and St. Cross *1973 (I-G), 1974*
Renton H J Eton College and Magdalen *1950, 1951*
Reynolds P J Uppingham School and St. Edmund Hall *1960, 1961*
Richmond C L St. Edward's School and Christ Church *1983 (I-G), 1984 (I-G), 1985*
Robertson B D University of Victoria Canada and Keble *1993*
Robinson N J Hampton School and Lincoln *1997, 1998, 1999 (I-G), 2000*
Roff P A V Melbourne University Australia and New College *1963*
Rogers J B Yale University USA and Balliol *1965 (I-G), 1966*
Rose D M Queensland University Australia and Balliol *1983 (I-G), 1984*
Rosengren G A M Harvard University USA and New College *1995, 1996 (I-G)*
Rowbotham J G Winchester College and Hertford *1958, 1959*
Rowe A D Eton College and Trinity *1948, 1949*
Roycroft J B Eton College and Keble *1996 (I-G), 1997, 1998, 1999 (I-G)*
Rubin R Yale University USA and Merton *1958*
Rutherford D C Rugby School and Magdalen *1959, 1960*
Said A Peshawar University and Pembroke *1957*
Saltmarsh P G Shrewsbury School and Keble *1967, 1968, 1969*
Sanders N W Radley College and Merton *1952*
Sawyier D R Harvard University USA and Christ Church *1973, 1974*
Scarlett J Y Eton College and Christ Church *1962*

Schuller P A A Harvard University USA and St. Catherine's *1993*
Screaton G R Trinity Hall Cambridge and Merton *1985 (I-G), 1986, 1987 (I-G)*
Searle J W C Hampton School and Christ Church *1988, 1989, 1990*
Sewall J O B Harvard University USA and Brasenose *1961*
Shaw D W Shrewsbury School and Keble *1959*
Shealy A W Harvard University USA and University *1977, 1978*
Sherratt J C D St. Edward's School and St. Edmund Hall *1961, 1962*
Skailes D S D Eton College and Keble *1962, 1963, 1964*
Slocock T G Shrewsbury School and St. John's *1989 (I-G), 1990*
Smith A J Melbourne Grammar School Australia and Merton *1951, 1953*
Smith J F E Eton College and New College *1951*
Smith M J Hampton School and St. Anne's *2000, 2001, 2002, 2003*
Snow D R St. Paul's School London and Balliol *1999, 2000, 2001*
Sorrell G St. Paul's School London and Christ Church *1955, 1957, 1958*
Spencer D C Yale University USA and Christ Church *1963, 1964, 1965*
Stearns A H Bedford School and Merton *1957*
Steel D W Eton College and Keble *1964*
Stewart G B Bournemouth School and Wadham *1986 (I-G), 1987, 1988*
Stewart J A G H Harrow School and Pembroke *1982 (I-G), 1983 (I-G), 1984*
Stoddart P G P Winchester College and University *1974*
Stokes L A F Winchester College and New College *1951, 1952*
Strong C M Shrewsbury School and Keble *1962, 1963*
Sutton T J Oundle School and St. Catherine's *1976 (I-G), 1977 (I-G), 1978*
Swayze T S Harvard University USA and Wadham *1960*
Tee N D C Emanuel School London and Balliol *1969, 1970, 1974, 1975*
Tennant T W Eton College and New College *1962*
Thomas A M S Winchester College and Pembroke *1984 (I-G), 1985, 1986*
Thomas M L Clifton College and Jesus *1952, 1953*
Thomson D G C Regent St. Polytechnic and Keble *1966 (I-G), 1967 (I-G), 1968*
Thorp R J Shrewsbury School and St. John's *1989, 1990 (I-G)*
Throndsen J-I UCLA USA and St. Peter's *1995*
Tinne N D Eton College and Keble *1962*
Topolski D Westminster School and New College *1966 (I-G), 1967, 1968*
Trippe E S Yale University USA and St. Edmund Hall *1965*
Turner C G Winchester College and New College *1951*
Turner Warwick R T Bedales School and Oriel *1946*
Vardey G E G St. George's School Weybridge and Balliol *1975 (I-G), 1977*
Venner B E B K St. Edward's School and St. Edmund Hall *1956*
Vine E V Geelong Grammar School Australia and Brasenose *1954, 1955, 1955*
von Ettingshausen C R D Dortmund University Germany and Keble *1999*

Ward A D The King's School Chester and Oriel *1986 (I-G), 1987*
Watson I A Shrewsbury School and Keble *1955*
Watts M W Westminster School and Oriel *1989 (I-G), 1990*
Weighell I R W Loughborough University and Hertford *2001*
Wells D P Stowe School and Magdalen *1955*
West D R King's College London and St. Catherine's *1996*
Westlake R G A Stowe School and Christ Church *1973*
Wheadon R A Cranleigh School and Balliol *1954*
Wiggins A J Wallingford School and Keble *1976, 1977, 1979*
Willis D R d'A Radley College and St. Peter's *1971, 1972*
Wilmer S E Yale University USA and Christ Church *1970*
Wilson J M St. Edward's School and Trinity *1953, 1955*
Wood J W Hampton School and Pembroke *1978*
Woodward W W Shore School NSW Australia and Brasenose *1948*
Wright P S T Hampton School and Oriel, *1974 (I-G), 1976 (I-G) 1977*
Yonge R P The King's School Canterbury and New College *1980 (I-G), 1981, 1982, 1983*
Young R C Bedford School and St. John's *1991*

CAMBRIDGE BLUES FROM 1946 TO 2003

Allen K St. C The King's School Canterbury and Magdalene *1991*
Allman-Ward M J Oundle School and Christ's *1946*
Almond H H Shrewsbury School and Lady Margaret *1950, 1951*
Ames R S N Eton College and 1st & 3rd Trinity *1987 (I-G), 1988*
Armstrong-Jones (Snowdon) A C R Eton College and Jesus *1950*
Arthur W T Witwatersrand University South Africa and Lady Margaret *1950*
Ashby J H Harvard University USA and 1st & 3rd Trinity *1966*
Ashton T R Monkton Combe School and Christ's *1949*
Ayer E D Harvard University USA and St. Edmund's, *1996, 1997*
Baart L W J Shrewsbury School and Caius *1979 (I-G), 1980, 1981*
Backhouse T Winchester College and Magdalene *1989*
Baillieu C L Radley College and Jesus *1970, 1971, 1972, 1973*
Baker M P Brown University USA and St. Edmund's *1993*
Ball J F E The King's School Chester and Robinson *1995 (I-G), 1996, 1997,*
Bangert D E Univ. of Wurzburg, Germany, and Lady Margaret *1992, 1993, 1994 (I-G), 1995*
Banovic M Northeastern University USA and St. Edmund's *1995*
Barnard G A D Lakefield College School Canada and Robinson *1983 (I-G), 1984, 1985*
Barnett M P C Harrogate Grammar School and Queens' *1994 (I-G), 1995, 1996*
Bartlett M H Radley College and Peterhouse *1957*
Barton C B R Millfield School and Jesus *1948*
Bathurst M D Merchant Taylors' Crosby and Pembroke *1977, 1978*
Baynes M G Bryanston School and Trinity Hall *1954, 1956*
Beckett M H Bedford School and Queens' *1963*
Behrens J H J Reading University and Downing *1992, 1993*
Berger S W Dartmouth College USA and 1st & 3rd Trinity *1983, 1984*
Bernstein I A City of London School and Emmanuel *1982, 1983, 1984 (I-G)*
Bernstein J A Harvard University USA and St. Edmund's *1993, 1994*
Bevan M V Bedford School and Downing *1963, 1964*
Beveridge J St. Paul's School London and Jesus *1959, 1960, 1961*
Bircher E A P Radley College and Christ's *1948, 1949, 1950*
Bliss N J Barnard Castle School and Corpus Christi *1981 (I-G), 1982*
Bracey A J L M University of East Anglia and Magdalene *1990 (I-G), 1991*
Bradley N C A Shrewsbury School and Pembroke *1974, 1975*
Breare R R A Eton College and Pembroke *1973 (I-G), 1976*
Brine P St. J St. Edward's School and Lady Margaret *1980 (I-G), 1982*
Brittin M J Hampton School and Robinson *1987, 1988, 1989*
Brooks S W Harvard University USA and St. Edmund's *2002*
Brooksby I A B Radley College and Lady Margaret *1965 (I-G), 1966*

Broughton P H Southampton University and Magdalene *1985, 1986, 1987*
Brown G H Shrewsbury School and Trinity Hall *1959, 1960*
Brownlee S A University of Canterbury, New Zealand, and St. Edmund's *1995*
Bruce J N St. Paul's School London and Clare *1954*
Buckmaster A C Charterhouse and Clare *1969 (I-G), 1970*
Budd H B Yale University USA and 1st & 3rd Trinity *1962*
Bull J G Royal Grammar School Newcastle and Emmanuel *1997 (I-G), 1998*
Burfitt N J Imperial College London and Emmanuel *1996*
Burnet N G Bedford School and Clare *1976 (I-G), 1977*
Burton Carole A The Alice Ottley School and Fitzwilliam *1986*
Butcher A S F City of London School and Queens' *1947*
Cadbury G A H Eton College and King's *1952*
Cadwalader G A University of Pennsylvania USA and Lady Margaret *1972*
Calder D W G St. Paul's School London and St. Catharine's *1961*
Cantwell R P Radley College and Peterhouse *1999 (I-G), 2000*
Carter M W J Rossall School and Pembroke *1965*
Carver A J R Eton College and Robinson 1994 (I-G), CUBC President 1996
Carver R D Eton College and 1st & 3rd Trinity *1958*
Cashin R M Harvard University USA and 1st & 3rd Trinity *1976*
Cassidy D J Shrewsbury School and Trinity Hall *1996 (I-G), 1997, 1998 (I-G)*
Challis C D C St. Paul's School London and Selwyn *1966 (I-G), 1967*
Chewton (Waldegrave) Lord J Eton College and 1st & 3rd Trinity *1962, 1963*
Christian M W Harvard University USA and 1st & 3rd Trinity *1961*
Christie A N The Leys School and Lady Margaret *1973 (I-G), 1975*
Christie D C Eton College and Pembroke *1958, 1959*
Church R C W The King's School Canterbury and 1st & 3rd Trinity *1968*
Church W E Eton College and 1st & 3rd Trinity *1965*
Clack N B M Wycliffe College and Lady Margaret *1952*
Clark E C Shrewsbury School and 1st & 3rd Trinity *1989 (I-G), 1990*
Clark M J S Shrewsbury School and Downing *1980 (I-G), 1981*
Clarke H G C Taunton School and Trinity Hall *1995 (I-G), 1996*
Clarke I R Ontario University Canada and Fitzwilliam *1986, 1987, 1989*
Clarke R J S Emanuel School London and St. Catharine's *1972*
Clarry N J John Hampden Grammar School and Jesus *1991, 1992, 1993 (I-G)*
Clay J H Eton College and Pembroke *1974, 1975, 1976*
Clayre I F C S Dean Close School and Queens' *1957*
Clegg S J Shrewsbury School and St. Catharine's *1977, 1978, 1979*
Coghill E J N T Gordonstoun School and Pembroke *1952*
Collier A J University College School London and Lady Margaret *1961, 1962*
Conze P H Yale University USA and 1st & 3rd Trinity *1966*

Cooke A V The King's School Chester and Jesus *1963*
Cooke-Yarborough A E Eton College and Caius *1977, 1978*
Cormack C A University College London and St. Edmund's *2001*
Corrie J R la T Winchester College and 1st & 3rd Trinity *1949*
Coventry K University of Melbourne, Australia, and Queens' *2003*
Cowderoy J A F The King's School Canterbury and Jesus *1981*
Cowie M P Cheltenham Grammar and Fitzwilliam *1981*
Crick J L M Marlborough College and Lady Margaret *1950*
Crombie R E B McGill University Canada and Peterhouse *1997, 1998, 1999*
Cross P W Cheadle Hulme School and Downing *1979*
Crowden J G P Bedford School and Pembroke *1951, 1952*
Cruttenden D L The Leys School and St. Catharine's *1969, 1970*
Cunningham P A British School of Brussels, Belgium, and Caius *1997 (I-G), 1998*
Dalley C J Winchester College and Queens' *1968 (I-G), 1969 (I-G), 1970*
Dalrymple A D Eton College and Downing *1979 (I-G), 1980, 1981*
Davey C J T Eton College and Jesus *1962, 1964*
Davies C M Bryanston School and Clare *1954*
Davies P B Tonbridge School and 1st & 3rd Trinity *1976*
Davies R N E Shrewsbury School and St. Catharine's *1977 (I-G), 1978, 1979*
Dawkins W M R Westminster School and 1st & 3rd Trinity *1976 (I-G), 1977 (I-G), 1978*
Daws C W Winchester College and 1st & 3rd Trinity *1968 (I-G), 1969*
Dawson-Bowling S J The King's Sch. Canterbury and Magdalene *1994 (I-G), 1995 (I-G), 1996*
de Giles P A Wellington College and Queens' *1948*
de Rancourt F G G Eton College and 1st & 3rd Trinity *1963*
Delafield P G R St. Edward's School and Jesus *1966, 1967, 1968*
Delahooke M G University College School London and Jesus *1956, 1957*
Denby A T Radley College and Magdalene *1958*
Denny J P M Downside School and Jesus *1956*
Dingle J R Christ's Hospital and Lady Margaret *1952*
du Bois P M Harvard University USA and 1st & 3rd Trinity *1955*
Duncan R P B Shrewsbury School and St. Catharine's *1972 (I-G), 1973, 1974*
Dunn R C E C Imperial College London and St. Edmund's *2001, 2002*
Earl D F Norwich School and Lady Margaret *1966 (I-G), 1967*
Eddy B M Carlisle Grammar School and Pembroke *1953*
Edwards-Moss T M Eton College and Lady Margaret *2001*
Ehlers R A Witwatersrand University South Africa and Lady Margaret *1998 (I-G), 2000*
Elliott J R Winchester College and 1st & 3rd Trinity *1995 (I-G), 1996*
Ellis D O M Harvard University USA and 1st & 3rd Trinity *1999*
Fawcett D N Harvard University USA and Magdalene *1992*
Fell J A Winchester College and Pembroke *1965*

CAMBRIDGE BLUES FROM 1946 TO 2003 continued

Fisher G H C Kingswood School and 1st & 3rd Trinity *1946, 1947*
Forster S F University of Dortmund Germany and Peterhouse *1998*
Fowler S L Eton College and Robinson *1990, 1991 (I-G), 1992*
Fraser J W Radley College and Jesus *1964, 1965*
Fraser R J Radley College and Jesus *1961*
Garman J R Shrewsbury School and Lady Margaret *1987, 1988, 1989*
Garner P J Bedford School and King's *1947*
Garrett J L D Shrewsbury School and Lady Margaret *1983, 1984, 1985*
Gibson E A F Queen's University Canada and Churchill *1986*
Giles J R Winchester College and Emmanuel *1958, 1959*
Gill C J Oundle School and Fitzwilliam *1967 (I-G), 1968*
Gillard D R Bedford Modern School and St. Catharine's *1991, 1992, 1993*
Glassman G J St. Paul's School London and Trinity Hall *1999 (I-G), 2000*
Gobbett J E St. Paul's School London and St. Catharine's *1961*
Gore S M Methodist College Belfast, and Jesus *1993, 1994*
Gosse J G St. Peter's College Adelaide Australia and Trinity Hall *1946*
Graham M E K Wycliffe College and Lady Margaret *1966*
Gray A H Shrewsbury School and Pembroke *1978 (I-G),1979*
Griggs Ellie L St. Paul's Girls School London and Robinson *2002, 2003 (I-G)*
Gritten M R Royal Military Academy Sandhurst and Queens' *1976*
Grundy N J St. Edward's School and Jesus *1986 (I-G), 1987, 1988*
Hall G F Tiffin School and Downing *1967 (I-G), 1968, 1969*
Hall P D Berkhamsted School and Corpus Christi *1953*
Hall-Craggs J F Shrewsbury School and Lady Margaret *1956*
Harpum R Royal Military Academy Sandhurst and Jesus *1976*
Harris G T Royal Grammar School High Wycombe and Jesus *1955*
Harris S A City of London School and Queens' *1982, 1983*
Harrison A B C Geelong Grammar School Australia and 1st & 3rd Trinity *1948*
Hart J A Hampton School and Fitzwilliam *1972*
Hart M J Hampton School and Peterhouse *1971 (I-G), 1972, 1973*
Haycock M N Abingdon School and Magdalene *1993, 1994*
Heard C D Shrewsbury School and Lady Margaret *1982, 1983, 1984 (I-G)*
Henderson G Radley College and Downing *1977 (I-G), 1978, 1979*
Henderson L M St. Edward's School and Selwyn *1966, 1967*
Hervey-Bathurst J F S Eton College and 1st & 3rd Trinity *1969 (I-G), 1970, 1971*
Heywood-Lonsdale T C Eton College and 1st & 3rd Trinity *1959*
Hill D K Shrewsbury School and Jesus *1954, 1955*
Hinde J F K Malvern College and Pembroke *1951, 1952*
Hirst L P University of Adelaide Australia and St. Edmund's *2000 (I-G), 2001, 2002*
Hobson P M Belle Vue Boys' School Bradford and Christ's *1984*

Höltzenbein P J M Ruhr University Germany and Magdalene *1994*
Hoffman M Harvard University USA and 1st & 3rd Trinity *1961*
Hole D E Foster's Grammar School and Selwyn *1988 (I-G), 1990*
Holmes P W Portora School and Lady Margaret *1960*
Hornsby N J Tonbridge School and Trinity Hall *1967, 1968, 1969*
Horton C M Eton College and Downing *1976 (I-G), 1977, 1978*
Hughes J D Bedford Modern School and Downing *1984 (I-G), 1985, 1986*
Hughes N G Winchester College and Queens' *1970, 1971, 1972*
Jackson B J R Witwatersrand University South Africa and Clare *1963*
Jacobs H R Winchester College and Pembroke *1972 (I-G), 1973, 1974*
James N W Latymer Upper School and Jesus *1971, 1972*
James T The King's School Chester and Trinity Hall *2003*
Jelfs A N de M John Mason School Abingdon and Fitzwilliam *1978, 1979*
Jennens D M Oundle School and Clare *1949, 1950, 1951*
Johnstone E T C Shrewsbury School and Lady Margaret *1960*
Jones J S M Shrewsbury School and Lady Margaret *1952, 1953*
Justicz D R M Harvard University USA and Downing *1992*
Justicz M C G Boston University USA and Sidney Sussex *1991, 1992*
Justicz N R T Brown University USA and Sidney Sussex *1989*
Kerruish S G I Eton College and Fitzwilliam *1970 (I-G), 1971, 1972*
Kiely J R Amherst College USA and 1st & 3rd Trinity *1964*
King J M Derby School and Lady Margaret *1953*
Kinsella J D Bedford Modern Sch. and St. Catharine's *1982 (I-G), 1983 (I-G), 1984, 1985 (I-G)*
Kitchin D J T Oundle School and Fitzwilliam *1975*
Kleinz M J Justus-Liebig-Universitaet Giessen Germany and Caius *2003*
Knight A R Hampton School and Clare *1982, 1983, 1984*
Lang I M Monkton Combe School and Caius *1947*
Langridge C Sir William Borlase's School and 1st & 3rd Trinity *1973 (I-G), 1974 (I-G), 1975*
Lapage M C Monkton Combe School and Selwyn *1948*
Laurie J H C Eton College and Selwyn *1980*
Lawes W R Tonbridge School and Pembroke *1966 (I-G), 1967*
Leadley D A T Bedford Modern School and Emmanuel *1953*
Lecky J M S University of British Columbia Canada and 1st & 3rd Trinity *1962, 1964*
Legget D F Radley College and Trinity Hall *1963, 1964*
Leggett G C M Portora Royal School and St. Catharine's *1967, 1968*
Lever J D Westminster School and 1st & 3rd Trinity *1971 (I-G), 1972 (I-G), 1973*
Lindsay K T Liverpool College and Jesus *1948*
Livingston J A Hampton School and St. Catharine's *2000 (I-G), 2001 (I-G), 2002, 2003*
Lloyd C B M Shore School NSW Australia and Lady Margaret *1949, 1950, 1951*
Loveridge S J Radley College and 1st & 3rd Trinity *1987 (I-G), 1988*

Lowe C M Shrewsbury School and Fitzwilliam *1969 (I-G), 1970*
Ludford G S S Latymer Upper School and Jesus *1949*
Lynch Odhams D V Westminster School and Jesus *1949*
Maasland J H St. Kentigern College Auckland New Zealand and Queens' *1963*
Macdonnell P L P Upper Canada College and Trinity Hall *1946*
Macklin D D Felsted School and Lady Margaret *1951*
MacLeod A L Shrewsbury School and Lady Margaret *1949, 1950*
Macleod J Bradford Grammar School and Lady Margaret *1973 (I-G), 1975*
MacMillan J R A Eton College and 1st & 3rd Trinity *1953*
Mallinson H Harvard University USA and St. Catharine's *2003*
Maltarp D P S Eton College and 1st & 3rd Trinity *1997*
Maltby M B Bedford School and Pembroke *1958, 1959*
Manser J P Westminster School and Sidney Sussex *1976, 1977*
Mant P M Cheltenham College and Selwyn *1988 (I-G), 1989, 1990*
Marshall G T Bryanston School and King's *1952, 1953*
Marshall M J Eton College and Jesus *1954*
Martin H N F De Montfort University and Trinity Hall *2000*
Mason W T M Shrewsbury School and Trinity Hall *1992 (I-G), 1993, 1994*
Masser K A Shrewsbury School and Trinity Hall *1954, 1955, 1956*
Massey P M O Oundle School and Lady Margaret *1949, 1950*
Maxwell D L Eton College and Jesus *1971, 1972*
Mayer S Albert Ludwigs University Germany and Caius *2002*
Mays-Smith A A M Eton College and 1st & 3rd Trinity *1955, 1956*
McCagg L B Harvard University USA and Emmanuel *1953*
McGarel-Groves A Eton College and Peterhouse *2001 (I-G), 2002 (I-G), 2003*
Meadows J R Yale University USA and Jesus *1957*
Mellows A P Monkton Combe School and Clare *1947, 1948*
Meyrick D J C Eton College and Trinity Hall *1947, 1948*
Milton R C Harvard University USA and Emmanuel *1957*
Monks R A G Harvard University USA and 1st & 3rd Trinity *1955*
Moore D P Geelong Grammar School Australia and St. Catharine's *1965*
Muirhead A R Trinity College Glenalmond and Lady Margaret *1955*
Muir-Smith M Sir William Borlase's School and Christ's *1964*
Murtough C B St. George's School Weybridge and Fitzwilliam *1968 (I-G), 1969*
Napier R A Winchester College and Lady Margaret *1962*
Neame J H Lincoln High School Oregon USA and Trinity Hall *1946*
Newton S B Radley College and Emmanuel *1992 (I-G), 1993 (I-G), 1995*
Nicholson R G Shrewsbury School and St. Catharine's *1961, 1962*
Nightingale M J H Tonbridge School and Trinity Hall *1956*
Norman T P A Harvard University USA and 1st & 3rd Trinity *1957*

CAMBRIDGE BLUES FROM 1946 TO 2003 *continued*

O'Loghlen J J Harvard University USA and Emmanuel *2000*
Omartian J D Harvard University USA and St. Catharine's *2003*
Owen J R Bedford School and Lady Margaret *1959, 1960*
Palmer J S Eton College and Pembroke *1979, 1980, 1981*
Panter M F Kingston Grammar School and Lady Margaret *1979 (I-G), 1980, 1981*
Parish M H W University of London and St. Edmund's *1994, 1995*
Parker J Shrewsbury School and Lady Margaret *1960*
Pasternak M L P Bradford Grammar School and Magdalene *1983 (I-G), 1984 (I-G), 1985*
Paton-Philip J S The Perse School and Lady Margaret *1946*
Pearson E M G The King's School Canterbury and Jesus *1982, 1983, 1984*
Peel S M The King's School Chester and Downing *1985, 1986, 1987*
Pepperell J C T Oundle School and Sidney Sussex *1986 (I-G), 1987 (I-G), 1988*
Perrins D J D Dauntrey's School and Jesus *1946*
Pew J S Stamford University USA and 1st & 3rd Trinity *1986, 1987*
Phelps R C Latymer Upper School and St. Edmund's *1993, 1994, 1995*
Phillips A G City of London School and Jesus *1979, 1980, 1981*
Phillpotts G J O St. Paul's School London and Clare *1970 (I-G), 1971*
Philp B M Bryanston School and Downing *1982, 1983, 1984 (I-G)*
Pim R J Methodist College Belfast and Downing *1996 (I-G), 1997*
Pitchford J A Tonbridge School and Christ's *1957, 1958*
Pooley G R Imperial College London and Lady Margaret *1988, 1989, 1990, 1991*
Potts A J University of Edinburgh and Trinity Hall *1996 (I-G), 1998*
Powell A F U Tiffin School and Pembroke *1974 (I-G), 1975*
Powell C S St. Paul's School London and Downing *1967 (I-G), 1968, 1969*
Price S R M Westminster School and 1st & 3rd Trinity *1960*
Pritchard J M St. Clement Danes School and Robinson *1984, 1985, 1986*
Probert A W N King's College London and Magdalene *1992*
Pumphrey C J Winchester College and Magdalene *1957*
Reddaway J H Oundle School and Fitzwilliam *1967 (I-G), 1968*
Redfern T M Shrewsbury School and Fitzwilliam *1969*
Reynolds A H Imperial College London and Pembroke *1984*
Richardson G C Winchester College and Magdalene *1947, 1948*
Rickett P D Eton College and 1st & 3rd Trinity *1958*
Ritchie R B Geelong Grammar School Australia and Corpus Christi *1958*
Roberts D J The King's School Chester and Lady Margaret *1965, 1966 (I-G)*
Robertson S N S Radley College and Fitzwilliam *1970*
Robinson P J Durham School and Lady Margaret *1975*
Robson C M Kingston Grammar School and Clare *1969*
Rodrigues C J University College School London and Jesus *1969 (I-G), 1970, 1971*
Rogers N S Brentwood School and Jesus *1947*

Ross R C The King's School Chester and Lady Margaret *1977, 1978, 1979*
Ross-Magenty (Blaettler) Lisa M Godolphin and Latymer and New Hall *1988 (I-G), 1990*
Russell J A L Marlborough College and Clare *1956*
Searle D J Radley College and St. Catharine's *1975 (I-G), 1976, 1977*
Sharif Vian Hampton School and Clare *1999*
Sharpley R F A Shrewsbury School and Lady Margaret *1951, 1952*
Shaw (Butler) Henrietta L Harrogate College and Lady Margaret *1985*
Sheppard P R W Durham University and Lady Margaret *1983*
Simpson A Bedford School and Queens' *1964*
Slatford R S Durham University and Hughes Hall *1995*
Smith B Hampton School and Trinity Hall *2003*
Smith G C D R University College London and St. Edmund's *1998, 1999*
Smith J H Winchester College and Caius *1974*
Smith M J K Shrewsbury School and Magdalene *1987 (I-G), 1988, 1989*
Smith R A B Shrewsbury School and Trinity Hall *1990 (I-G), 1991, 1992 (I-G)*
Spink R A B Sherborne School and Downing *1987, 1988*
Sprague D B Durham School and Emmanuel *1973 (I-G), 1974*
Staite R J Evesham and St. Catharine's *1989 (I-G), 1990, 1991, 1992 (I-G)*
Stallard T A Oundle School and Jesus *1999, 2000, 2001, 2002*
Stanbury R G Shrewsbury School and Lady Margaret *1964, 1965*
Stancliffe J C G Harrow School and Pembroke *1954*
Stephens R J King's College School London and Emmanuel *1980 (I-G), 1981, 1982*
Stokes R P Shrewsbury School and 1st & 3rd Trinity *1998 (I-G), 1999 (I-G), 2000*
Story A P Henley College and St. Edmund's *1997, 1998*
Streppelhoff T Ruhr University Germany and St. Edmund's *1994*
Sturge D P Radley College and Lady Margaret *1973*
Sulley J S Radley College and Selwyn *1958, 1959*
Sullivan B A The King's School Chester and Selwyn *1971*
Sullivan T J Oundle School and Clare *1946*
Swainson C J C St. Edward's Sch. and Fitzwilliam *1999 (I-G), 2000 (I-G), 2001, 2002, (I-G)*
Sweeney M A Becket School and Lady Margaret *1965, 1966*
Tanburn J W Charterhouse and Jesus *1954*
Taylor R D Shrewsbury School and Trinity Hall *1993 (I-G), 1994, 1995*
Tebay M D King's College School London and 1st & 3rd Trinity *1966, 1967 (I-G)*
Thomas G C Shrewsbury School and Jesus *1946*
Thompson R J M Radley College and Pembroke *1957*
Thompson-McCausland B M P Eton College and 1st & 3rd Trinity *1959*
Tollemache, J N L Eton College and 1st & 3rd Trinity *1962*
Tourek S C Dartmouth College USA and 1st & 3rd Trinity *1973, 1975*
Tozer S G D Winchester College and 1st & 3rd Trinity *1955*

Travis Q R L C Winchester Coll. and Downing *1984 (I-G), 1985 (I-G), CUBC President 1986*
Tweedie D J St. Paul's School London and Trinity Hall, *1999 (I-G) 2000*
Vernon J J Radley College and Trinity Hall *1955*
Walker D J Bootle School and Clare *1974*
Wallace T J King Edward VI School Southampton and Jesus *1997 (I-G), 1998, 1999*
Waller R M Emanuel School London and Downing *1995 (I-G), 1996*
Wallis J A N Bryanston School and Lady Margaret *1953, 1954*
Walmsley R Fettes and Queens' *1962*
Ward R G Charterhouse and Queens' *1965, 1966*
Waterer R A Radley College and Sidney Sussex *1977, 1978 (I-G), 1979 (I-G)*
Waters III S R University of Pennsylvania USA and 1st & 3rd Trinity *1971*
Watson A R Cavendish School and Sidney Sussex *1996 (I-G), 1997*
Webb P J Monkton Combe School and Queens' *1963*
Webber M O'K The King's School Canterbury and Jesus *1973*
Weber M Technische Universitat Germany and St. Edmund's *1998*
Weiss Leigh Harvard University USA and Emmanuel *1989*
Welch S T University of Technology Australia and St. Edmund's *2002*
Wells M P Aylesbury Grammar School and Selwyn *1975 (I-G), 1976*
Welsh I W Shrewsbury School and Queens' *1956*
West A J Yale University USA and Caius *1999, 2000, 2001, 2002*
West K M Dulwich College and Christ's *1998 (I-G), 1999, 2001*
Weston R T Dulwich College and Selwyn *1960, 1961*
Wheare H J H Magdalen College School and Jesus *1973 (I-G), 1974*
Whitney T W Harvard University USA and Jesus *1980*
Whyman K King's School Chester and Peterhouse *1996, 1997*
Wiggins F P T University College School and Lady Margaret *1960*
Wigglesworth C J Bryanston School and Jesus *1980, 1981*
Williams M D Oundle School and Trinity Hall *1972 (I-G), 1973*
Wilson M Princeton University USA and Trinity Hall *1986*
Winckless R N Tiffin School and Fitzwilliam *1967, 1968, 1969*
Windham W A D Bedford School and Christ's *1947, 1951*
Witter J S Pangbourne College and St. Catharine's *1983 (I-G), 1984 (I-G), 1985*
Wolfson J M Eton College and Pembroke *1987*
Woodhouse J W Shrewsbury School and Selwyn *1978 (I-G), 1980*
Wooge T Northeastern University USA and Peterhouse *1999, 2001, 2003*
Worlidge E J Marlborough College and Lady Margaret *1951*
Wright A J King Edward VI School Norwich and Corpus Christi *1990, 1991*
Yarrow R D Durham School and Lady Margaret *1966 (I-G), 1967*
Young R C Bedford School and Downing *1989, (I-G), 1990*
Yuncken T F Melbourne University Australia and Pembroke *1974*

Oxford versus Cambridge from 1829

*1912 first race, both sank
*1951 first race, Oxford sank
*1998 record

The first race was from Hambleden Lock to the bridge at Henley-on-Thames. Races 2 to 6 were from Westminster to Putney. The rest were rowed from Putney to Mortlake except in 1846, 1856 and 1863 when the race was held on the ebb tide from Mortlake to Putney. There were two races in 1849.

	YEAR	WINNER	TIME	DISTANCE
1	1829	Oxford	14.30	Easily
2	1836	Cambridge	36.00	60 seconds
3	1839	Cambridge	31.00	1.45 minutes
4	1840	Cambridge	29.30	3/4 length
5	1841	Cambridge	32.30	1.5 minutes
6	1842	Oxford	30.10	13 seconds
7	1845	Cambridge	23.30	30 seconds
8	1846	Cambridge	21.05	3 lengths
9	1849	Cambridge	22.00	Easily
10	1849	Oxford	–	Foul
11	1852	Oxford	21.36	27 seconds
12	1854	Oxford	25.29	11 strokes
13	1856	Cambridge	25.45	1/2 length
14	1857	Oxford	22.50	32 seconds
15	1858	Cambridge	21.23	22 seconds
16	1859	Oxford	24.40	Cambridge sank
17	1860	Cambridge	26.05	1 length
18	1861	Oxford	23.30	47 seconds
19	1862	Oxford	24.40	30 seconds
20	1863	Oxford	23.06	45 seconds
21	1864	Oxford	21.40	27 seconds
22	1865	Oxford	21.24	4 lengths
23	1866	Oxford	25.35	3 lengths
24	1867	Oxford	22.39	1/2 length
25	1868	Oxford	20.56	6 lengths
26	1869	Oxford	20.04	3 lengths
27	1870	Cambridge	22.04	1 1/2 lengths
28	1871	Cambridge	23.10	1 length
29	1872	Cambridge	21.15	2 lengths
30	1873	Cambridge	19.35	3 lengths

	YEAR	WINNER	TIME	DISTANCE
31	1874	Cambridge	22.35	3 1/2 lengths
32	1875	Oxford	22.02	10 lengths
33	1876	Cambridge	20.20	Easily
34	1877	Dead-Heat	24.08	Dead-Heat
35	1878	Oxford	22.15	10 lengths
36	1879	Cambridge	21.18	3 lengths
37	1880	Oxford	21.23	3 3/4 lengths
38	1881	Oxford	21.51	3 lengths
39	1882	Oxford	20.12	7 lengths
40	1883	Oxford	21.18	3 1/2 lengths
41	1884	Cambridge	21.39	2 1/2 lengths
42	1885	Oxford	21.36	2 1/2 lengths
43	1886	Cambridge	22.30	0.67 lengths
44	1887	Cambridge	20.52	2 1/2 lengths
45	1888	Cambridge	20.48	7 lengths
46	1889	Cambridge	20.14	3 lengths
47	1890	Oxford	22.03	1 length
48	1891	Oxford	21.48	1/2 length
49	1892	Oxford	19.10	2 1/4 lengths
50	1893	Oxford	18.45	1 length 4 feet
51	1894	Oxford	21.39	3 1/2 lengths
52	1895	Oxford	20.50	2 1/4 lengths
53	1896	Oxford	20.01	2/5 length
54	1897	Oxford	19.12	2 1/2 lengths
55	1898	Oxford	22.15	Easily
56	1899	Cambridge	21.04	3 1/4 lengths
57	1900	Cambridge	18.45	20 lengths
58	1901	Oxford	22.31	2/3 length
59	1902	Cambridge	19.09	5 lengths
60	1903	Cambridge	19.33	6 lengths
61	1904	Cambridge	21.37	4 1/2 lengths
62	1905	Oxford	20.35	3 lengths
63	1906	Cambridge	19.25	3 1/2 lengths
64	1907	Cambridge	20.26	4 1/2 lengths
65	1908	Cambridge	19.20	2 1/2 lengths
66	1909	Oxford	19.50	3 1/2 lengths
67	1910	Oxford	20.14	3 1/2 lengths
68	1911	Oxford	18.29	2 3/4 lengths
69	*1912	Oxford	22.05	6 lengths
70	1913	Oxford	20.53	3/4 length

	YEAR	WINNER	TIME	DISTANCE
71	1914	Cambridge	20.23	4 1/2 lengths
72	1920	Cambridge	21.11	4 lengths
73	1921	Cambridge	19.45	1 length
74	1922	Cambridge	19.27	4 1/2 lengths
75	1923	Oxford	20.54	3/4 length
76	1924	Cambridge	18.41	4 1/2 lengths
77	1925	Cambridge	21.50	Oxford sank
78	1926	Cambridge	19.29	5 lengths
79	1927	Cambridge	20.14	3 lengths
80	1928	Cambridge	20.25	10 lengths
81	1929	Cambridge	19.24	7 lengths
82	1930	Cambridge	19.09	3 lengths
83	1931	Cambridge	19.26	2 1/2 lengths
84	1932	Cambridge	19.11	5 lengths
85	1933	Cambridge	20.57	2 1/4 lengths
86	1934	Cambridge	18.03	4 1/4 lengths
87	1935	Cambridge	19.48	4 1/2 lengths
88	1936	Cambridge	21.06	5 lengths
89	1937	Oxford	22.39	3 lengths
90	1938	Oxford	20.30	2 lengths
91	1939	Cambridge	19.03	4 lengths
92	1946	Oxford	19.54	3 lengths
93	1947	Cambridge	23.01	10 lengths
94	1948	Cambridge	17.50	5 lengths
95	1949	Cambridge	18.57	1/4 length
96	1950	Cambridge	20.15	3 1/2 lengths
97	*1951	Cambridge	20.50	12 lengths
98	1952	Oxford	20.23	Canvas
99	1953	Cambridge	19.54	8 lengths
100	1954	Oxford	20.23	4 1/2 lengths
101	1955	Cambridge	19.10	16 lengths
102	1956	Cambridge	18.36	1 1/4 lengths
103	1957	Cambridge	19.01	2 lengths
104	1958	Cambridge	18.15	3 1/2 lengths
105	1959	Oxford	18.52	6 lengths
106	1960	Oxford	18.59	1 1/4 lengths
107	1961	Cambridge	19.22	4 1/4 lengths
108	1962	Cambridge	19.46	5 lengths
109	1963	Oxford	20.47	5 lengths
110	1964	Cambridge	19.18	6 1/2 lengths

	YEAR	WINNER	TIME	DISTANCE
111	1965	Oxford	18.07	4 lengths
112	1966	Oxford	19.12	3 3/4 lengths
113	1967	Oxford	18.52	3 1/4 lengths
114	1968	Cambridge	18.22	3 1/2 lengths
115	1969	Cambridge	18.04	4 lengths
116	1970	Cambridge	20.22	3 1/2 lengths
117	1971	Cambridge	17.58	10 lengths
118	1972	Cambridge	18.36	9 1/2 lengths
119	1973	Cambridge	19.21	13 lengths
120	1974	Oxford	17.35	5 1/2 lengths
121	1975	Cambridge	19.27	3 3/4 lengths
122	1976	Oxford	16.58	6 1/2 lengths
123	1977	Oxford	19.28	7 lengths
124	1978	Oxford	18.58	Cambridge sank
125	1979	Oxford	20.33	3 1/2 lengths
126	1980	Oxford	19.20	Canvas
127	1981	Oxford	18.11	8 lengths
128	1982	Oxford	18.21	3 1/4 lengths
129	1983	Oxford	19.07	4 1/2 lengths
130	1984	Oxford	16.45	3 3/4 lengths
131	1985	Oxford	17.11	4 3/4 lengths
132	1986	Cambridge	17.58	7 lengths
133	1987	Oxford	19.59	4 lengths
134	1988	Oxford	17.35	5 1/2 lengths
135	1989	Oxford	18.27	2 1/2 lengths
136	1990	Oxford	17.22	2 1/4 lengths
137	1991	Oxford	16.59	4 1/4 lengths
138	1992	Oxford	17.44	1 1/4 lengths
139	1993	Cambridge	17.00	3 1/2 lengths
140	1994	Cambridge	18.09	6 1/2 lengths
141	1995	Cambridge	18.04	4 lengths
142	1996	Cambridge	16.58	2 3/4 lengths
143	1997	Cambridge	17.38	2 lengths
144	*1998	Cambridge	16.19	3 lengths
145	1999	Cambridge	16.41	3 1/2 lengths
146	2000	Oxford	18.04	3 lengths
147	2001	Cambridge	19.59	2 1/2 lengths
148	2002	Oxford	16.54	3/4 length
149	2003	Oxford	18.06	1 foot
150	2004			

Bibliography and sources

Books

The following books provide information on the Boat Race. They are given in date order. We gratefully acknowledge information contained in these books, though we have tried to use contemporary accounts so far as this has been possible. For biography and history related to the boat race, Christopher Dodd's The Oxford and Cambridge Boat Race (1983) contains a more extensive bibliography. Since its publication, several club histories have been published containing information about the exploits of blues, notably Geoffrey Page on Thames (Hear the Boat Sing, Kingswood Press, 1991), Geoffrey Page and Richard Burnell on Leander (The Brilliants, Leander Club 1997) and Eric Halladay on Rowing in England: a Social History (Manchester University Press, 1990). Dodd's The Story of World Rowing (Stanley Paul, 1992) contains a comprehensive rowing bibliography. Several publications followed Oxford's mutiny of 1987, notably The Last Amateurs by Stephen Kiesling in the New Yorker (14 March 1988), True Blue by Daniel Topolski with Patrick Robinson (Doubleday, 1989), and its riposte, The Yanks at Oxford by Alison Gill (The Book Guild, 1991).

1870
Oxford and Cambridge Boat Races
by WF MacMichael, London, Deighton Bell

1883
Record of the University Boat Race 1829–1880 and of a commemoration Dinner 1881, by GGT Treherne & JHD Goldie; London; Bickers & Sons

1900
The Story of the Inter-University Boat Race
by Wadham Peacock and Grant Richards

1909
The Record of the University Boat Race
1829-1909 and register of those who have taken part in it. CM Pitman, London; T Fisher Unwin. Updated from Treherne & Goldie

1929
The University Boat Race: Official Centenary History (with register of Blues) by GC Drinkwater and TRB Sanders; London; Cassell & Co

1929
One Hundred Years of Boat Racing
(official centenary souvenir) 1829-1929, by William Wimbledon Hill; The Albion Publishing Co.

1939
The Boat Race by GC Drinkwater; Blackie & Son

1954
The Oxford & Cambridge Boat Race 1829-1953
by RD Burnell; Oxford University Press.

1956
The Boat Race by Gordon Ross;
The Sportsman's Book Club

1979
One Hundred and Fifty Years of the Oxford and Cambridge Boat Race by Richard Burnell, Precision Press/Guinness; with supplement 1980.

1983
The Oxford and Cambridge Boat Race
by Christopher Dodd, London; Stanley Paul/Hutchinson.

Boat Race media coverage

Regatta magazine publishes the programme and an account of both races in the issue following the race. The British Rowing Almanack also contains an account of the boat race and, usually, the Isis-Goldie race with the statistics. Errors creep into both from time to time.

Most of the quality press published extensive accounts and analyses of the pre-race training with lithograph and later photographic illustrations throughout the nineteenth century. In recent years the cover has been reduced, but the commentary, normally by rowing correspondents with extensive experience and knowledge, is still excellent. Reports on the Monday morning after the race give a good account of it, but it is unusual to find other than the result of the Isis-Goldie race.

The BBC has broadcast radio commentaries since 1927 and television commentaries from 1949 to 2004. Archive radio recordings are rare, but the two university clubs and the River and Rowing Museum at Henley hold video copies of just about every race from 1949, which are available for study purposes by prior arrangement.

Contributors

Duncan Clegg Rowed for Oxford 1965, 1966 (President). London Representative of Oxford and Cambridge Boat Clubs 1984-2004. Merchant banker turned company director.

Christopher Dodd Writer and journalist. Author of The Oxford and Cambridge Boat Race (1983). Curator of Battle of the Blues exhibition. Rowing correspondent of the Guardian from 1970 to 2002, currently with the Independent.

Mark Edwards Boatbuilder and specialist in traditional craft.

Donald Legget Rowed for Cambridge 1963, 1964, Goldie 1962. Coach at Cambridge since 1968, with prime responsibility for Goldie since 1991. Rowing correspondent of the Observer 1966 to 1970.

Dr John Marks Boat Race statistician and joint author of The Bumps (2000). Honorary treasurer of Cambridge University Boat Club 1986 to 1998 and 2000. Honorary senior treasurer of Cambridge University Women's Boat Club 1977 to 1991.

Hugh Matheson Rowed for Oxford 1969. Member of Oxford coaching team 1973 to 1985 and 1987. Chairman of the Oxford University Boat Club Trust Fund from 1993, director of P to M Ltd from 2000. Businessman and journalist. Rowing commentator for Eurosport.

Barbara Slater Head of General Sports, BBC. Producer of the Boat Race coverage for BBC television 1999-2002. Member of British Olympic gymnastics team, 1976.

Mike Sweeney Rowed for Cambridge 1965 and 1966 (President). Member of Cambridge coaching team from 1969 to 1980. Umpired the Boat Race six times between 1984 and 1998. Chairman of the Boat Race Umpires' Panel from 2002. Chairman of FISA Events Commission from 1990. Chairman of Henley Royal Regatta from 1993.

Daniel Topolski Rowed for Oxford 1967, 1968, Isis 1966. Oxford coach 1973 to 1987 and 1995 to 1997. Coaching advisor from 1997. Writer, broadcaster and motivational speaker. Author of Boat Race: the Oxford Revival and True Blue: The Oxford Boat Race Mutiny (with Patrick Robinson).

Robert Treharne Jones IT consultant, journalist and sometime general practitioner. Member of Radio 5 commentary team from 1989, timekeeper on radio launch.

Thomas E Weil Collects rowing memorabilia and lectures and writes on rowing history when not practising law. Wishes he could have gone to Oxford or Cambridge after Yale instead of Vietnam. Trustee of River and Rowing Museum.

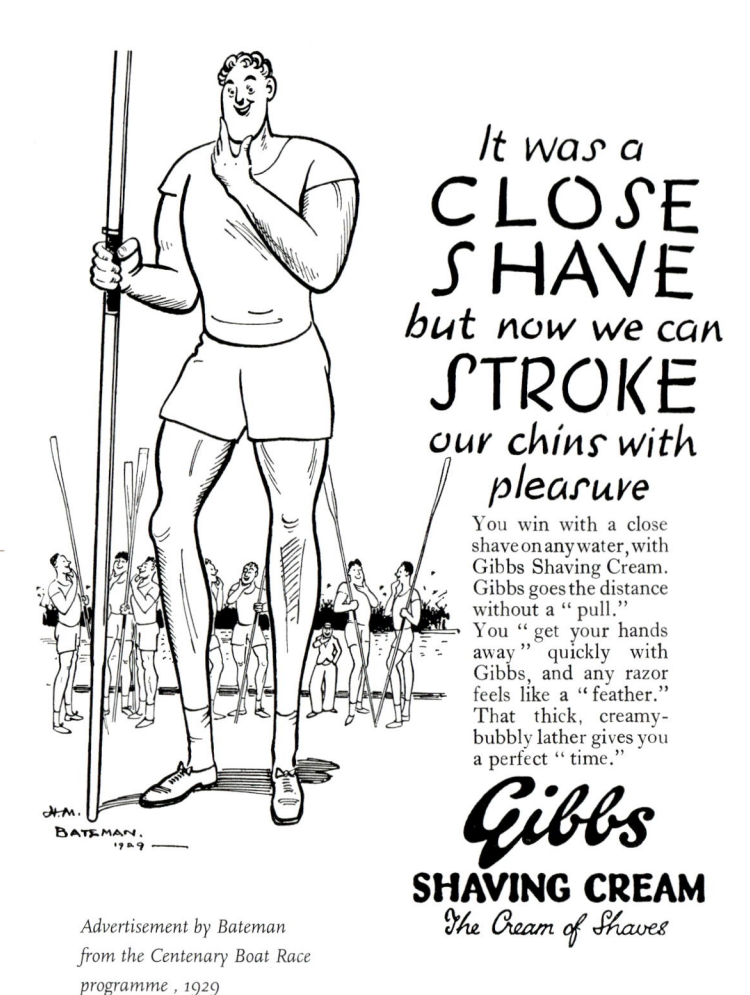

Advertisement by Bateman from the Centenary Boat Race programme, 1929

Colophon

Battle of the Blues

First published in 2004 by P to M Limited, Midway House, 27-29 Cursitor Street, London EC4A 1LT

© 2004 Christopher Dodd and John Marks

For illustration copyrights see illustration and photographic acknowledgements on reverse of back cover flap.

The right of Duncan Clegg, Christopher Dodd, Mark Edwards, Donald Legget, Hugh Matheson, John Marks, Barbara Slater, Mike Sweeney, Daniel Topolski, and Thomas E Weil to be identified as authors of the work has been asserted by them in accordance with the Copyright, Designs and Patents Act 1988.

All rights reserved. No part of this publication may be reproduced, stored in a retrieval system, or transmitted, in any form or by any means without the prior written permission of the publisher, nor be otherwise circulated in any form of binding or cover other than that in which it is published and without a similar condition being imposed on the subsequent purchaser.

A catalogue record for this title is available from the British Library

Design + production O'Reilly Richardson, London
orr@bvillage.demon.co.uk

Origination + printing BAS Printers Ltd, Salisbury

The Oxford & Cambridge University Boat Clubs are most grateful to KPMG who supported the creation of this book which celebrates the 175th anniversary of the first (Oxford & Cambridge) boat race.

KPMG

Editors' acknowledgements

For their insights of a private affair in the public eye, Duncan Clegg, Mark Edwards, Donald Legget, Hugh Matheson, Barbara Slater, Mike Sweeney, Daniel Topolski, and Thomas E Weil.

Special thanks to Thomas Weil for free rein amongst his extensive collection of boat race imagery and ephemera, and to the River and Rowing Museum for access to its library, archive and image collection.

Photographers Jaap Oepkes, John Shore and Peter Spurrier for delving into their dark rooms, George Gilbert for his invaluable database of boat race detail and Robert Treharne Jones for additional information.

The following for research and leg-work carried out with alacrity: John Adamson, Tom Barry, Susan Brown, Diana Cook, James Felt, Ditte Hviid, Tom Jenkins, Hugh Laurie, Julia Lindsey, Paul Mainds, Eamonn McCabe, Sam McLennan, Wayne Pommen, Dominic Reid, David Riches, Christopher Rodrigues, Mike Rosewell, Michael Rowe, David Searle, Suzie Tilbury, Dobs Vye, Richard Way.

Last but not least, the Blues of Oxford and Cambridge University Boat Clubs for making history, and the directors of P to M Limited for making this book possible.

Right: 'Here they come', a view off Chiswick from The Graphic, 1890